ADVANCE PRAISE

"'I like a hitch in the line, like you— / my little art is doubling, too,' writes Maurice Manning, and *Plume Poetry 10* doubles the reader's pleasure. Rhyme's basis is the companionship of sound and sound, and the companionship of poet and poet is the basis of this anthology. Its structuring principle is as inspired as the poems that comprise it. Familiar names invite unfamiliar ones, so the joy of recognition alternates with the joy of discovery. You get to see where the art is and where it is headed. Mark Irwin's kinetic translations of Arthur Rimbaud show us still other kinds of poetic companionship—that of poet and translator, and of the dead and the living. This anthology is the perfect companion for every lover of American poetry."

– Amit Majmudar

"Way back whenever, the newcomer among us is said to have turned up with a sealed letter of introduction: My Dear Monsieur Bigger-Britches-Than-Most: the one bearing this message is named _____, knows how to _____ quite well and, by my lights, is definitely worthy of your attention. I guarantee this individual will add to memorable conversation at your table, thus deserving at least one good meal.

"A century or two beyond, we have more meaningful generosity: the *Plume* anthologies, now this most wonderful #10 where Bob Hicok welcomes Karan Kapoor, Martha Rhodes walks with Rushi Vyas, Carol Muske-Dukes singles out Yona Harvey. Plus we find thirty-nine other remarkable pairs who startle and give solace. This is a unique show-me-the-goods volume in a share-the-wealth, we-aren't-Shakers mode so that life-saving poetry goes on in spite of horrific threats to stop it—Covid, climate change, racial injustice, possible nuclear annihilation. Not that recognized poets far longer on the wheel have an understanding much greater than those at work still largely under the radar or writers who have recently taken it up, the real work; only that belief in those new or relatively new to poetry is crucial to its rich and continuing bloodline.

"That is to say: bravo Danny Lawless, for keeping the cup moving and alerting us to joy, sorrow, wry and earnest witness to poetry's many-layered right now. Which takes us out of time with a raised glass into future time.

"And I almost forgot: Rimbaud rocks (again, again, again)."

– Marianne Boruch

"Someone once asked Tennessee Williams what younger playwrights he admired. He replied, 'Honey, I'm too old to cover the waterfront.' Being old myself, and no longer teaching, I sometimes feel overwhelmed by the sheer volume of poetry out there. So many poets, so little time! I've come to rely on these inventive *Plume* anthologies, which are double-curated, first by Plume's choice of established poets (an extremely various bunch), and then by those poets' choice of younger or lesser-known poets, so the range of work is enormous. Many of these writers are completely new to me, and I doubt I'd ever have come across them otherwise. I find many of them to be truly original, by which I mean not that they say things never said before (though they often do), but rather that the work goes back to the origins of its perceptions, allowing us to see how a poem's meaning comes into being. I look for that quality in poems, and find it here in abundance. This collection is like a big plate of irresistible hors d'oeuvres."

– Chase Twichell

"From the very beginning, I've loved the spirit of discovery and advocacy that lives in every volume of the *Plume* anthology. In this big tenth anniversary offering, that spirit lives on. Here, forty-two (!) established poets offer not only their own new work but also introduce us to the work of great poets we may not yet know. Here, also, Mark Irwin has done fine work complicating the life and work of

Rimbaud through his own research and his translations of Rimbaud and Borer. There is simply so much good poetry here, such a sense of literature as a shared endeavor among writers, readers, translators and editors. And so many wise conversations arise in these pages. It's a joy that *Plume* has made it ten years. This annual anthology's gift to American readers is enormous."

– Kevin Prufer

plume poetry 10

plume poetry

10

edited by
DANIEL
LAWLESS

Featured Poet Arthur Rimbaud

Essays, Letters, Photographs, and New Translations
by Mark Irwin and Alain Borer

Canisy Press

Alan Shapiro • Emily Banks
Alejandro Escudé • Allen C. Jones
Andrei Codrescu • Radu Vancu
Ani Gjika • Olivia Banks
Beckian Fritz Goldberg • Miguel Murphy
Bob Hicok • Karan Kapoor
Carol Moldaw • Nathan McClain
Carol Muske-Dukes • Yona Harvey
Cecilia Woloch • Grażyna Wojcieszko
Clare Rossini • Kai-Lilly Karpman
Daisy Fried • Glorious Piner
Dan O'Brien • Ananda Lima
David Wojahn • Adam Grabowski
Elena Karina Byrne • Cathy Colman
Flávia Rocha • Ruy Ventura
Garrett Hongo • Alycia Pirmohamed
Gerry LaFemina • Madeleine Barnes
Gregory Orr • Safiya Sinclair
Jane Hirshfield • Danusha Laméris
Jeffrey Skinner • Ann Townsend
Jennifer Franklin • Michelle Whittaker
Jim Daniels • Julie Heming
Juan Felipe Herrera • J.J. Hernandez
Kelli Russell Agodon • Katerina Canyon
Kwame Dawes • Romeo Oriogun
Linda Bierds • Elizabeth Bradfield
Lynn Emanuel • Deborah Bogen
Maggie Smith • L.A. Johnson
Martha Rhodes • Rushi Vyas
Maurice Manning • Nathaniel Perry
Michael Waters • Yesenia Montilla
Nicole Callihan • Zoë Ryder White
Nin Andrews • Cassandra Atherton
Rae Armantrout • Brandom Som
Rafael Campo • Stacy Nigliazzo
Ramón García • Ata Moharreri
Shamar Hill • Carolyn Joyner
Sophie Cabot Black • Tacey Atsitty
Steven Cramer • Aaron Wallace
Timothy Donnelly • Julia Burgdorff
Tom Sleigh • Karen Fish
Ye Mimi • Wu Yu Hsuan
Sarah Luczaj
Steve Bradbury

Featured Poet: Arthur Rimbaud

L'Œuvre-vie et la métanoia d'Arthur Rimbaud
Arthur Rimbaud's Life-work and Spiritual Quest
by Alain Borer
Translated from the French by Mark Irwin. ALL RIGHTS RESERVED.

PHOTOGRAPHIC CREDITS:

page 107 | Close-up from Arthur Rimbaud [c. 1872]—foto de Étienne Carjat

page 108 | Self-portrait of Arthur Rimbaud in Harar, Ethiopia in 1883 . Thanks to Alain Tourneux, président des Amis de Rimbaud (ancien conservateur du musée Rimbaud de Charleville)

page 126 | Self-portrait of Arthur Rimbaud aboard ship in Harar, Ethiopia; sent to his family in a letter posted the 6 of May 1883. Thanks to Alain Tourneux, président des Amis de Rimbaud (ancien conservateur du musée Rimbaud de Charleville)

Published by Canisy Press

Printed in the United States of America
First Printing, 2022
Printed by Bookmobile, Minneapolis, MN

ISBN 978-1-7325956-3-7

Library of Congress Control Number: 2022936932

Cover and book design by I Libri Book Design

If, indeed, per Prévert,

«Le jardin reste ouvert pour ceux qui l'ont aimé»

to all who have had a hand in this, along the way.

CONTENTS

FEATURED POET • ARTHUR RIMBAUD

INTRODUCTION

Readers, hello!

The above my usual salutation, as you may recognize, yet this time . . . somehow different: a decade now passed since our first anthology! How to describe this . . . feeling? As if like some huff-puff middle-aged adventurer I've somehow finally managed to clamber to a foothold on an obscure but beautiful mountain, that seemed so much smaller in the brochure. Or perhaps think of a party, the *best* party, the kind you're nervous about at first, alone in a new city, haven't really been invited to, but by evening's end one at which you find yourself relaxed in a way you'd never believe possible, making friends, drinking Mai Tai's with what seems like the whole block, everyone fascinating, gifted, offering without reserve or guile the name of a *fabulous* club, this or that artist *you really must meet.*

Anyway, different.

Although—to revert to the matter at hand—not because anything has objectively changed: *Plume Poetry 10* remains much as its predecessor left it: a collection of poems from forty-two "established poets" along with those of a selected "less well-known" partner (I really must think of other descriptors), and a short introduction by the former to the latter. Nor, as with *Plume Poetry 9*, have we altered our hopes for a greater diversity of subject and perspective, while retaining the highest standards of craft.

No, any divergence lies in me, alone. Again, this is our tenth anniversary. That's practically three quarters of a century in literary journal age. And, let's face it, even with the magic tricks of WordPress and jpegs, email and social media, it's not always easy, especially for one as inept as I in these matters. Don't get me wrong. I'm not complaining. Unlike in the early years, I now have a staff both stellar and dependable, and the good offices of the Shifting Foundation (thank you, **David Breskin** and **Chelsea Hadley**) have afforded me much-needed help in layout—our resident wizard, **Christina Mullin**. Still, there are moments . . . a late arriving or abruptly cancelled contribution, the scourge (and blessing, yes) of Submittable. Neither, I realize, am I alone in this minor purgatory: every editor I have been fortunate to meet, one way or another tells me so.

All to say, while I know *Plume* online will endure as long as I can manage it the future of the print anthologies is less clear. Finances, or lack thereof (the Shifting folks have been generous but even their inhuman patience must know its limits), play a part, of course—materials and production costs rise each year, and anthologies are notoriously a hard sell. But, who knows? It's quite possible this is simply age or the flickering embers of fatigue; on the other hand, no wants to be Willie Mays at 42, losing a routine high fly—in Shea Stadium.

In the meantime, before I leave you to the poems only a page or two away, let me thank those who so eminently deserve it: **Jason Cook, Robert Archambeau, Marc Vincenz, Adam Tavel, Mary Bisbee-Beek, Kristen Weber**, to say nothing of that indispensable staff: **Nancy Mitchell, Leeya Mehta, Amanda Newell, John Ebert, Joseph Campana, Amy Beeder, Chard deNiord, Mark** and **Chelsea Wagenaar, Sally Bliumis-Dunn, Mihaela Moscaliuc**—and so many more.

For now, then, let's—let us—just say, we do hope you enjoy the book!

Daniel Lawless
Editor, *Plume*

plume poetry 10

Alan Shapiro

Emily Banks

How an idealistic child can fold American aggrandizement, competitiveness and vanity into a charitable intention that reinforces if not perpetuates the injustices she's trying to address is one of the delicate ironies of this disquieting poem. In its acknowledged complicities and self-indictment, "Charity" is driven by political emotion, not political opinion, which is why it offers no easy answer to the troubles it confronts.

ALAN SHAPIRO

Street Walker

> "... and we talked of the wretched life of such women."
>
> —Boswell

No "stubborn stays," no bustle, your petticoat
so draggled and flimsy that it yields the shape
it covers, as, now, two men arm in arm, approach,
two easy marks, you might be thinking, though
it's the older one you choose, the uglier,
with his scrofula-riddled wattle of a neck, his face
a pock marked swarm of twitches—so distracted,

you could pick his pocket and get clean away
before he even gets the chance to touch you,
except, no sooner do you smile in his direction
than his finger's up and wagging, and he's saying
not ungently, "No, no my girl, it won't do,"
and they walk past, lamenting the wretched fate
of girls like you. And so your cameo is over.

The one trace left of you. Everything else
before and after this page's flash of failed enticement—
has utterly vanished, as Johnson's ugly face
has vanished, his pockmarks and tics, his shabby
finery and fob you can't get close enough to pick.
Listen: though you're no Ninon, and I'm no Johnson,
you're my girl now, on this page. You serve my pleasure,

my bawdy cynosure of being gone, embodying
for me a vanishing so absolute I can't escape
the thought of it or think it, that I too will be
where you are, and Johnson is, and Boswell, where
all our endless pettifogging ends must come to, sooner or later,
"bound up, hitched up, tight laced, painted, scented,
or besmirched, in silk or wool, with or without sugar."

EMILY BANKS

Charity

When my third-grade Gifted Program class
at P.S. 29 in Cobble Hill
learned about the *crisis in Kosovo*,
we wanted to do something. I announced
a stoop sale for the refugees. Back then,
we assumed a little good old fashioned
American consumerism would fix everything.
That morning, after Jennifer arrived, Ariel called
to say Aarian was over at her house and they'd decided
to move the sale there—she had more room.
She lived in a brownstone with two polished floors,
whereas my home was mostly hallway, raw
and full of splinters. I refused to leave.
We taped price tags to all my parents' junk,
years of unsorted treasures Ariel's neat shelves
could never yield. We advertised
in sidewalk chalk, waited on the steps
to tell passersby about Milosevic and ask
if they would like to buy an old toy shopping cart
or a troll doll, a miniature castle or a book of maps.
My father made chocolate milkshakes,
as many as we requested, and we chugged
them till our throats went cold. We raised
over twice as much as the other girls did.
Beating them was my favorite thing
about saving ethnic Albanians.
I was my country's daughter, craving
the slick revenge of victory, basking
in the fantasy of my own hardscrabble ambition
filling the mouths of every refugee.

Alejandro Escudé
Allen C. Jones

In "Exile's Kitchen: Breaking Things," Allen C. Jones writes about his insecurities as an American immigrant living in Norway. I use that word "immigrant" on purpose because it's what I understand. Originally from Argentina, having moved to the United States at the age of six, I get it when Allen writes that his hands are "brutal" and that everywhere he looks there are "shattered things." This is what it feels like to be out of place. It's an existential feeling that is wonderfully captured by this gifted writer. Allen and I were roommates in college. I like to think I "introduced" him to poetry, but I think the positions have reversed now. By enduring a similar transplantation to the one I went through, Allen has now found the mature voice of an artist. Allen's "brutality" is what gives him that special knack for seeing the bluntness he so wittingly describes in this poem. That "blunt" nature is the same energy as Lorca's duende, Wordsworth's "recollection," and Whitman's "song." These are all one thing. Few poets have access to this energy. Sure, there are many poets who win awards and publish title after title, but they are mere "precise machines," something the narrator in this poem ironically laments no longer having access to.

ALEJANDRO ESCUDÉ

The Woman I Never Saw Coming

The truth is more painful than the truth these days.
Everybody is a flying monkey. Everyone an immortal squirrel.
I visit the dentist to find friends. They put my front crown back on,
the one that cracked off at McDonald's; I used my teeth
to open a plastic bag with a toy in it, my daughter's request.
I hope there's no longer a sick mouse coiled up in my chest.
I woke up to the drunken stupor in which most people talk,
the plans they make, the moving they do, fanatics with a broken
    brain-bone.
My broken friend holds his coffee with both hands as if it's holy.
Mother phones to tell me not to leave my apartment with the
    dishwasher on.
When you're tired of life, it's called depression, and no one allows you
to be tired of life, except where money isn't required and money's
    required
wherever you go—except where there is poetry. That's why
we're always craving poetry. But no one gives us poetry
because poetry is the most expensive commodity, save love.
I want a Trevi Fountain love. I want Grecian beauty. I found it in her.
When I'm with her, the man green-eyeing me from next table
becomes a lovable jerk. The corner couple rooting for me to fail
become film extras who won't receive a speaking role.
I brush my pink horse under a blue sky. There are no flaws
in this woman's written Spanish. She returns from the restroom
wearing maroon lipstick. With both hands, she pulls back
her lush, brown-black hair, and I swallow my breath.

ALLEN C. JONES

Exile's Kitchen: Breaking Things

I once marveled at my ability to catch things. Wine glasses, knives, a
heart. I recall a day when it rained dishes. I dried each and put it in
its place, my hands machines of indifference, leaping out of their own
accord to snatch the fallen from their timeline. I now marvel at their
clumsiness, blunt, bullheaded things that have turned against me,
making up for all those years of obeisance. I can barely pour a drink
without killing someone. Today, cursing my brutal hands, worried the
downstairs neighbor might hear me destroying my life, I marveled at
the incredible circumference of shattered things. I swept high and
low, in rooms I hadn't used in years and closets I didn't know existed.
Everywhere invisible slivers had taken root, a well-groomed lawn of
invisible blades. To think I once walked barefoot. Tired of cutting
myself at every step, I purchased steel-soled boots, eyed every lover
like a candy-covered razor, cleaned so deeply I was sure nothing would
ever break again. Thank god this was all years ago in a far-away town
made solely of ice. And though I never left, I am walking barefoot
again, banging my blunt fists against everything, giddy with the happy
violence of a house so clean it has ceased to exist. So today, as I put the
last of your things in the trash, it surprised me to feel a shard slide deep
into my heel. I dropped to the floor, stupidly caressing myself, my hands
trembling with nostalgia for the precise machines they once were.

Andrei Codrescu

Radu Vancu

Radu Vancu, translator of the complete Ezra Pound into Romanian, is an erudite encyclopedist. He also writes a poetry aware of a world in need of tender and authentic human sensibility. In a rich poetic landscape, his voice insists that beauty exists and "Nothing, and this is no big talk—nothing can push us further."

ANDREI CODRESCU

Postpandemic Manifesto

Craziness rules, but poetry is currency.
Poets oppressed by Cyberia rise!
Your are free labor for the maw of capital
and the egos of hustlers!
Starting now every word is worth $3745.
The barely imaginative of now are NFTing the OED.
The barely imaginative of the past already dot-com'ed
the OED, the Webster and all the dictionaries.
Much water flowed under the Rouge River since Marianne Moore
named a car in Detroit. Many waves of the Seine
passed over the suicides of Paul Celan and Gherasim Luca.
Careless over Hart Crane pass the currents under the Brooklyn Bridge.
There is no longer any real estate left either in Cyberia or in Hades.
Only the inarticulate sounds you utter in your sleep between screens
and nightmares and the combos of letters are truly yours
because you don't remember them
and only what isn't remembered can't be bought.
Forget everything
write nothing down
let poesy flow through you like the Seine the East River
all words must commit suicide before they can be sucked
by the merchants of the internet who feed on our slave sweat.
Poets of the world you must shatter the screens for fair wages.
This assigner must pay $749,000.
I will throw in the title and my name for lagniappe.

RADU VANCU

from *Psalms,* Casa de editură Max Blecher, 2019

Master of children's small fingers
& of the indestructible hair of girls
& of the transparent shields of the gendarmes—

today I saw videos of children with broken heads
& fingers broken, I saw girls dragged by their shiny
& indestructible hair by gendarmes with shields transparent

as your indestructible light, I saw
indestructible teeth broken, indestructible bodies
shattered, I saw the blood made by you

splattering in the world made by you
& there was still so much beauty in it
& it is exactly this that mashes me.

Any amount of beauty mashes me.
An indestructible beauty in a world blown into pieces—
your cynicism is divine, indeed.

I saw a dog licking the bleeding face
of his mistress, collapsed under the boots of the gendarmes,
careless to their blows which also crushed his ribs.

He wagged so happily his tail
when she raised her grazed hand & patted him,
there was so much indestructible light around him,

for him the evil only passed accidentally through the world.
A cop with a high visor, a blond & pure child,
came running & hit her again.

Master, I sometimes tell myself you only passed accidentally
through the history of the world you made, just as we pass
only accidentally through the poems we write.

And that it is of your indestructible & luminous beauty
that the hardest transparent shields are made.
And that the happiest of us are wagging our tails,

licking the bleeding faces of our loved ones. Mashed
under the boots of the seraphim rapid intervention units.
Terrorized by the anti-terrorist units of the angels.

Who to endure so much beauty
—and until when
—and why.

You unbelievably gentle master, if I wouldn't feel sometimes
your harsh tongue licking my bleeding brain,
if I wouldn't see your furry tail sometimes

wagging happily—everything would be easier
& more unbearable. Don't worry, we're talking here
between indestructibles.

Ani Gjika

Olivia Banks

Olivia Banks' poetry is hypnotic and addictive in the way that poems which describe individual identity in the process of wrestling with obsessions, desires, and beauty can often be that. Some of her sentences are masterfully built so that nothing can be added to them or removed. This is because she doesn't keep things from the reader, but she also only keeps the door of interpretation ajar and wants the reader to probe and discover, something which I've always found rewards many rereadings of my favorite poems and inspires me to write my own in turn. While Banks uses bare bones kind of language, stripped of complex syntax and ornate details, her sentence structure surprises and many lines stick with you. Listen, for example, to the cadences in these lines: "But I'm glad she turned me into nothing so I / knew I was something" or "Still, she touched my body so carefully that night—like it was a cemetery full of dead fathers" as well as the last two sentences in this poem.

The speaker only alludes to traumas and the form of the poem itself—a collage of sorts, and a collage within a collage—serves to inform the reader of this crucial information. I admire how the poem opens with the words "I don't know why" and ends with knowing "this is the last time." The speaker comes full circle through different relationships from being someone who chose partners that weren't fully present for her to someone no longer waiting to be claimed by an other, the way she knows she can no longer wait for the loss of a father, in time, to have any less weight. I can't wait to see her debut poetry collection come out one day soon!

ANI GJIKA

This Pandemic, Breathing

I turn myself on my back, remove the bed covers and take off my shirt.
My breasts already awake, their mouths waiting like little birds to
    be fed
and my hands feed them as I run them over, under,
pulling on one nipple, pulling on them both.
Unlike so many things in my life I've arrived late at,
I've always mothered my desire.

Earlier, I took off my clothes to get in the shower.
I'm a little older than my mother was the day when she must have
    gone out
to get groceries and I found myself folding and putting away her
    clothes.
I must have been five or six, maybe seven,
the same age I've been when all my life happened to me.
I folded her shirts and with each fold she was right there. Her scent
    was—
sweet-wet earth, crushed rose petals, tar cloud, talcum powder
though she never wore any—the scent of hard work
and an entirely unselfconscious young woman who made sure she
was present for everyone else: husband, two children, a mother-in-law,
and a ten or twelve hour shift.

Standing in front of the mirror in my bathroom, lifting my arms
to pull my shirt off, for the first time, my armpits smelled like my
    mother's
so many years ago. I smelled them again the way you return to hug
    a friend
you know you won't see for a while.
I tell the mother in my memory: "I'll always remember you like this—
forever youthful—live in me!" and get in the shower.

I have never seen my parents have sex. I have never asked my mother
if she's ever enjoyed it. Now, under the covers I remember how
    one night
a man rolled over to kiss me but stopped and breathed in so deeply
when face to face with my armpit I knew the animal in him.
And it's this same animal of my body I'm here with tonight.
I don't even have to do anything more than pull on these red mouths
for all the little mouths all over my body to tell me yes. Yes,
says my navel and twitches when I press on one of these birds, I think
    she smiles. Yes
escapes my mouth and hovers over me like a firefly. Yes,
behind my neck and under my ears, and deep within, a louder pulse,
or maybe the temperature of my own blood answers back yes, yes,
and somewhere even deeper where I don't even need to locate it
because it is so far inside me it's already the center of the universe,
I feel a lift off, and the entire ride I'm an explosion of yes, yes, yes stars,
my body a mirror reflecting only light. I breathe.

OLIVIA BANKS

Girls

I still don't know why K pretended we were
strangers the last time we saw each other.
But I'm glad she turned me into nothing so I
knew I was something. It's been years since
we stopped pretending to see stars in the
suburbs and I still wonder if she meant what
she said that night on her front porch.
Because I meant it every time I drove on the
wrong side of the road just to make her
laugh.

I hate that B kissed me at the end of our date
when I didn't want to be kissed. I hate that
she pinched my waist when she pulled me
into her and said *I wish I could wear jeans
like that.* I wish I had told her to get off me.
I wish I had told her *what you really want is
a body that denies itself.*

A and I met in treatment. She was there
because she made herself bleed. I was there
because I hadn't bled since the funeral. The
first night I slept at her apartment, she kept
asking me what I wanted until it wasn't
about what I wanted anymore. So I stared at
the ceiling and let myself become nothing
but a back to bite into and when it was over
I whispered *to be honest, A, I just wanted
someone to listen.* She climbed off me with a
drunken sigh and said *trying to love you is
like living in a hospital.*

On the drive to her house, S told me to
ignore the car seats in the back of her car and
the gray in her roots so I did. When she
asked me how old I was, I told her the truth
but added three years so she would think I
was hotter. Still, she touched my body so
carefully that night—like it was a cemetery
full of dead fathers.

When C got mad

(at me) and broke   things the
shards of

glass

stayed on her floor for days I wasn't
allowed
to pick
them up
she wanted   to wallow in
the   hurting   she
said it was   art
so I left the

glass
there   and her bed
became an island
where I slept in my
makeup

and faced   the wall

I tried again with R. She bought me a donut at 2 AM after her birthday party and we kissed on someone's front lawn, cigarette smoke swirling in the space between our throats. R didn't even know how to kiss: I had to cup her face gently and say *here. Do it like this.* She asked me if she should keep her eyes closed and I said *yes* and she said *but I want to see you when I do it because you're* and I said *Don't.* Then I pulled away and asked if she was out yet. She said *no. Not yet.* A layer of dew quivered inside her eyes as she tried to hold my hand. But I put it in my pocket and said *this is the last time.*

Beckian Fritz Goldberg
Miguel Murphy

Miguel Murphy's poems combine the cinematic, an unbridled lyricism and delicious diction with relentless probing of the human interior. The poem "Sunlight" opens quietly as the speaker begins a meditation on "the blue middle of my life." The quiet opening belies the poems real subject which is hunger, rendered as a drama of the poem's natural elements, water and fire/light. The "wolfish" starlings give way to to a lyric riff on a match flame in the speaker's hands as he evokes a moment from Tarkovsky's film *Nostalghia* where the protagonist Gortchakov attempts to fulfill a promise to walk across the pool of St. Catherine carrying a lit candle. "What is desire" the poet asks, "if not this burden." Beautiful in its intensity, Murphy transforms the natural elements into the self's "inner theater" with compassionate insight.

BECKIAN FRITZ GOLDBERG

Autumn in California

for Bruce

A deer was swimming in the surf
half mile out near Dana Point

people on the beach pointed
sea doe
nostrils stung with brine

carried over the blue green green
blue swell
toward some desire beyond

genus, until some long-boarder
guided her back to shore, dying

wave gleaming like an eye,
the sunlight, the sand-mirror—

Where do you go
when you go?
Who called you?
Lucky I'm the age when I don't
expect answers.

The deer took off running
down the beach and bounded
back into the water

an almost perfect day
robin's egg sky
little wind
out there so little between
ecstasy and desperation,

What do you want
in the heave of a wave,
your hooves walking on water?

How is it to live your whole life
without a word—

Until you just start swimming.

MIGUEL MURPHY

The Sunlight

You wouldn't know it could feel so redundant—
the wolfish starlings plunder the grass
and nothing burns. Big Sur. We came here to rest.
The coast, a color. The thought of nothing,
the blue middle of my life—
                          A cliff side and a footpath
down to the small beach. And fire, there
a cold wind. Long waves the whole year—restless,
leafy and metallic,
                      the brightness of ash. The sunlight
like something from Tarkovsky, one pointless, small ambition
in which passion turns into a terrifying tenderness. Deep
cargo in the hull; heartache. And somehow you knew
you should light the match, like a person condemned
to whom the starlight is
another brief monument to what
                         is fallible. Your life,
little fireling, little warlike starling, flickering indignantly, all
erotic umbrage. Broken wing in my hand. Pathological, shy
flame, I will care for you. Little shape of my fate, my
certain failure. What
                  is desire, if not
this burden. Dearth and glut
cupped in your hands: wild, deadheaded, and blue.

Bob Hicok

Karan Kapoor

Karan reads poems to the Ganges. The Ganges carries them downstream and plants them in the earth. The earth grows flowers that look like mouths. Lonely people kiss the flowers and feel wanted. Karan's name comes from the Sanskrit word "karna," which means ears. His name is a good listener and his poems help me hear a world that I recognize but don't inhabit. All of our worlds are like that, populated by exactly one person stuck between what they have and what they believe they are missing. I love this table, that it holds the full weight of how Karan sees his father. I love the chasing and the following light. I love lists and I love this list for staying true to itself and for changing as it goes. The book of ruins should be everyone's bathroom reading. I am sitting here wondering why the best poems appear to have written themselves.

BOB HICOK

Yet again, again

When a man beats a man to death, he has time to stop.
For example, between punching, tasing, punching, cuffing,
shackling, tasing, kicking, punching, tasing, choking,
kicking, tasing, tasing, punching, standing on, punching,
tasing, punching, punching, tasing, punching, punching,
punching, kicking, choking, and complaining about all the blood
he was getting on them, the cops who also dragged Ronald Greene
face-down and left him prone for nine minutes to suffocate
under his own weight, could have stopped at any point
and smoked a cigarette or had a heart transplant or wondered
if god or the moon would approve of beating a man to death
for his skin. Eve doesn't want to watch the video,
Weston doesn't, Karim, my mom, my cat won't, the maple can't,
and I feel stupid that I can't breathe in an out simultaneously
like a bird, that I can't find that ease and fluidity
or write a poem that makes men like this put their fists down.
They worked him over for about an hour. In an hour
I could move several yards of dirt or watch an episode
of *Law and Order* in this universe or *Law and Disorder*
in an alternate universe or meditate for sixty times as long
as I've ever meditated in my three hundred attempts combined
or read 2008's anemic and unpoetic H.Res 194
three hundred and twenty times, including congress'
"commitment to rectify the lingering consequences
of the misdeeds committed against African Americans
under slavery and Jim Crow and to stop the occurrence
of human rights violations in the future." From the future
I can ask the past, how's that going for us?
They had time to stop and debate the definition
of first-degree murder and I've had time to stop
knowing what to say about this shit
except that we've had time to stop and debate
if a society that lets this happen over and over
isn't a society that wants this to happen over and over,

and I'm not great at breathing if you ask a bird
or haberdashery if you force me to remember what that is
but I'm aces at noticing that we could have prosecuted
the fuck out of people like this and locked them up
until rapture came and god said "I don't want 'em, you keep 'em,"
but we didn't and don't and this means
that you don't need a rope to lynch a man: you need a badge.
As long as that sentence is true,
I don't see a way forward in America, a way toward the America
America wants to see in the mirror. Maybe apologizing
is what makes us human, more than darts and electric cars
and art, than all the Taj Mahals and Under Pressures
put together, and we never have, we white to black,
not genuinely officially or sufficiently, not with pomp
and circumstance and cash, not proficiently for whips
and chains and brands and rapes and illiteracy,
for red-lining and poll-taxes and tests and crack,
and all the rest, all the all that surrounds us every day,
the two Americas you see if you drive through any big city
from top to bottom, east to west. When a country tries
to beat a people to death, it has time to stop.
We need actions that speak louder than nooses and guns
and love for all our daughters and sons. Civil people
don't deny but apologize for their mistakes, seek to mend,
not rend, offer an open hand, not a fist, and ask forgiveness
by acts of repair. The only way to set the burden of slavery down
is to pick it up. We never have. Not really. Not like Germany
did the Holocaust and do you really want that comparison
to stand? The dumb fucks were mad at Ronald Greene
for getting the blood they beat out of him all over them.
Seriously insane in the membrane. You can't make this shit up
and don't have to in a country that's made an art
of such lunacy for four hundred years.

KARAN KAPOOR

The Table

My father comes home a few minutes after midnight. He puts the keys to his shop and motorcycle on the table. He takes off his helmet and puts it on the table. All the light that came in as he opened the door—some of it chasing him, some of it following—he collects all of it without prejudice and puts it on the table. Hoping for relief, he deposits his knife, anger and fog next to the light. He opens his hands and the rivers which flow out of his palms find rest on the table. He takes out a pack of gold flake from his pocket and tosses it in the colossal river. On Tuesdays he brews his dreams for dinner—shaking his head, he spills them on the table. He lays out on the table his sleep and the table does not creak. He unchains his old watch, inherited from his father, and docks it beside a puddle of sweat. He takes off his shoes and socks, picks up the book of ruins from the table, and walks to the bathroom. I am standing here wondering how the table looks so clean.

Carol Moldaw
Nathan McClain

Nathan McClain's first book, *Scale*, is an interrogation of losses, of their moment by moment—momentous—consequences. He is a careful poet, in multiple senses of the word: attentive, painstaking, full of cares, caring. Which is not to say there are not flights of fancy, agile linguistic escapades, and quick escapes. When he lays out a train of thought, we don't know where it will lead, but we do know that it will be alert not just to what is seen, but to what is "shifting, unseen, all around you."

In three-line stanzas of mostly three-beat lines, "I could hardly tell" delicately enacts a journey of recognition and identification through touch and the imagination. It begins with an admission of unknowing, "I could hardly tell / one tree from another." Knowing here begins with touch, "the way / one might search for a pulse"—for a life-force—the beat of a poem—where the trunk is scarred. So far, everything is straight-forward, "as one might expect," but here the poem enlarges: in touching the scar, the speaker not only imagines the boy "flashing his pocketknife," but feels a deeper influence on them both, "the tree's rhetoric // or perhaps the permanence of affection," which makes him "feel nearly kin" to the once indistinguishable tree. Touch has turned into feeling; ignorance into kinship—and that lovely, mysterious, phrase, "the tree's rhetoric," stays and resonates.

CAROL MOLDAW

Radical Acceptance

Yes, I say back, affirming that I too
cherish our recent heart-to-heart, although
I suspect the reference is to a talk
we never had. It doesn't matter to me
that our hallowed conversation is supposed.
It's meaningful enough to stand in for
other talks we didn't have or botched.
I'm not a word person, she often said,
usually in response to my questioning
whether some phrase I thought misused
expressed quite what she intended to say.
That we were at odds over issues of speech
aggravated—aggrieved, I think—us both
until the truce-like terms her brain imposed.

NATHAN McCLAIN

I could hardly tell

one tree from another
until, up close, I touched
the trunk, thick, gnarled

as one might expect, with
two fingers—the way one
might search for a pulse—

where the bark had been badly
scarred not by a woodpecker
but by young lovers—the boy

flashing his pocketknife—
persuaded, as even I
have been, of the tree's rhetoric

or perhaps the permanence
of affection, so in some way,
one could feel nearly kin to it.

Carol Muske-Dukes
Yona Harvey

This just in—to add to her awards—Yona Harvey was just announced as a 2022 Guggenheim Fellow in poetry!

Years ago, when I introduced Yona Harvey (along with her former partner) at a very special USC Library reading celebrating both poets—I already knew her poems on the page and had been powerfully affected by them. (Hence my invitation to her to read!) Of course, hearing the poems in her musically resonant voice, I had the same Emily Dickinson, "top of the head" sensation that I'd experienced reading poem after poem in her debut book, about to be published back then. Yona took her time. (She has never jumped at the spotlight.) Through the timing of the measured build-up to the lightning-quick revelations in her poems the reader connects to the velocity of her style.

Readers seek out her poems and never forget their landscapes of both dream and unrelenting reality. I cannot forget her poems, and have written about them in the past, as I'm doing now, as the poems keep presenting new ways of being differently aware. Yona Harvey's poems deserve more: by which I mean more readers, more witnesses to lines like: "I've trembled / among strangers / & lovers turned strangers." She has called her voice "small and solitary" when in fact her voice is wide-ranging and ecstatic as "gospel, a loose shell in a tambourine, waiting for rapture."

Yona Harvey's two books, *Hemming the Water* and *You Don't Have to Go to Mars for Love*—have won awards like the Kate Tufts Discovery Award, a Barbara Deming Award (and now a Guggenheim)—and her bold originality has propelled her into a whole other sphere—she is the first Black woman to write for Marvel comics and the first Black woman to write for the Marvel character, Storm.

There is no other poet like Yona Harvey, the lightning preceding the storm, the lightning within.

CAROL MUSKE-DUKES

Notes on an Informer

Tiny idol, glib two-faced Janus
Of the shut door, micro-chip slice
Of listening mirror. You are earring

Size, quarter implant. Covered
Tracks, sniper silence, all fail to
Stunt your pomp: pimp high style.

Fake-safe in your own smug habitat,
That promiscuous dark park of failed
Imagining: where you fill up "Self"

At the pedagog pump. Vestal learners
Of your "art" get taught to tart it up. All
This double business: embroidering with

Purple thread on the bodies of the dead:
Your own style a toy coffin of fin-de-siecle
Stained satin. You're so busy above it all,

Saving your own skin, through fulltime parry
And thrust, though the sabre in your gnat-grasp
Feigns a tripped rigor, like a stiff's—after a final

Breath. At critical mass, you divest yourself of
Evidence—under a bridge where buried cables
Snake, then swivel up to the surface, spot-lit.

Damning reports X-out your busy prints.
Charges, redacted, zero in on unwitting
Targets, while you lie abed, writing on Conscience,

Its stolen crown sliding outsize on your skull.

YONA HARVEY

Frog District: Origins

I zipped my wetsuit & flopped
from the edge of a queen-sized bed,
into the deep; which is to say I turned
in my sleep & swam to the pond
where no one recognized me, away
from the faithless & careless, toward
the skulls of monks who ground
their jawbones & moaned:
*We're born & we die. We once swam
where you swim.* Excuse me? Had I
needed reminding? More
amphibian than queen, more mad
than merry, the after-anger of frog work
treaded inside me. I had netted fish, I had
scrubbed algae, I had shaken the speckled remains
of food from lava-colored castles.

All you had to do was ask, whispered
unlifted fingers. Bubble talk.
But let me not trouble those waters.
My story leaps elsewhere, spider-webbed
emerald-eyed, post-weary. I kick
my way back top. Bye-bye, Froggy
Bottom. Keep your convenient book
of procedural treasures, your lectures
above the wellsprings, your bit of

eerie swampland & half-breed
mermaids wrecking toy ships.

Cecilia Woloch
Grażyna Wojcieszko

It was poetry that brought me to Poland in the first place, but that's another story. What's kept me coming back, over the course of twenty-five years of annual sojourns—beginning in the mid-1990s and extending into the present—have been my friendships with poet-translators like Grażyna Wojcieszko and Sarah Luczaj, which have provided me with sustenance and inspiration.

The poem of Grażyna's I've chosen to share, in Sarah's translation, is from a multi-part, book-length work entitled *Incantation*. I hope that this piece of it, a single poem entitled "Blue Day," can offer a sense of the larger work's sweep and strangeness and power.

On the one hand, *Incantation* seems to be a sequence of lyrical, imagistic poems, accumulating into a kind of narrative, interspersed with shifting lists of things for sale—animals, fields, machinery—is there anything, ultimately, not for sale?

On the other hand, it seems to be a long poem composed almost wholly of the unsaid, pointing to the strange gaps in our knowledge of the world and to our equally strange relationship with nature — in other words, to our estrangement.

Or is it a kind of fairytale? Reading the poem evokes both terror and enchantment; the poem is brutally straightforward, yet infused with tenderness. The poet's radical empathy with animals, with plants, with what one Polish critic has called "the fate of the smallest, eternal inhabitants," is utterly transformative.

Grażyna Wojcieszko's is a unique and compelling voice—European, transnational, transgressive, combining intelligence and passion, restraint and outrage, fusing an intimate familiarity with the natural world with a keen perception of the uses and abuses of technology. I wasn't surprised to learn that her education includes studies in artificial intelligence as well as agriculture. I find her poems visionary, apocalyptic, and achingly romantic.

CECILIA WOLOCH

Weather

Then it was suddenly winter again. Then it was summer, then spring. Some mornings were molten gold in the trees and some evenings were bitter and without stars. And these were the same days, some days, on the earth. Flood and fire and drought; rats in the square before the cathedral and, in the cathedral, rats—breeding year-round, in multitudes. *What would Jesus do*, some asked? What would Christ say from their holy books? Or Allah or Buddha or any god? Some made of food an elegant art; many went hungry, made homeless by war. There was a gun for almost every hand, whole arsenals underground. There were rivers filled with poison ash and towers of mirrors, made all of glass. Some mornings we woke and walked through wind so sharp, so clear it hurt.

GRAŻYNA WOJCIESZKO translated by SARAH LUCZAJ

Blue day *from Incantation*

Yurek
the sea is talkative today
it's having a talkative blue day
and the waves brought in a stormy
rabble

on the beach a shocked herring
shocked that it's not working
its just not working for him at all
swimming

his mouth won't shut
his mouth won't shut and his lips
flap in the wind and remember
something

his tail records on the sand
on the sand it writes of the stomach
of the eaten-up bowels
of the liver

it gazes with an astounded eye
an ever paler eye
it looks at the misty world
and the sky

the sky is azure blue today
he has an azure blue day of indecision
he doesn't know what to do what to do
with his memories

Clare Rossini

Kai-Lilly Karpman

In the fall of 2019, Kai-Lilly Karpman was a student of mine in a senior poetry workshop at Trinity College. The class was small—six students—and we met in the living room of an old house on campus for three hours at a time: long, leisurely sessions during which the class grew close in a familial way. Kai came in having read and written a good deal of poetry, and went at her work with a kind of ferocity that I rarely see at the undergraduate level. She had, and has, a questing spirit. The poems in her final portfolio were electrifying, at times, disturbing. Some delved into sex and sexuality, including poems about an abusive relationship with an older man. Others took on political subjects: wetlands destruction, the displacement of indigenous peoples. But Kai was equally capable of approaching subjects less loaded: the character of an elderly aunt, the midwestern landscape, animals she'd known and loved.

After graduating from Trinity in 2020, Kai went into an MFA program, where she continues to write her brilliant, fiery poems. "Grover" arrived in a sheaf of recent work. The poem's opening—"I'm thinking of my Mother's childhood dog...."—has a relaxed intimacy, hardly preparing us for what follows. The image of the maggots eating the dog alive is profoundly disturbing, yes, but no less so than the fact that this same universe contains such delicacies as a child on a scooter and a cathedral which "wears a peaceful face." The remonstrance in the final line is tonally rich; I wouldn't attempt to reduce it to an adjective. "Grover" presents Kai-Lilly Karpman as a young poet with the courage to measure both ugliness and beauty, in language that mitigates neither. How not to feel thrilled by the possibilities inherent in such work?

CLARE ROSSINI

That Beach You Went to Last Night

—Did its waves flounder at your feet?
And what of our perfectly round moon, drawing itself up
like some flower trumpeting over dirt?
I know you saw it.
Nineteen, sunburned, you take your music through pods
nestled deep in your ears, voices
keeping voices away.
You say I ask too many questions.
But dawn impinges, and your youth is bound to fail.

Last night, I dreamed of waking, soaked with blood
as you began your exit of my body,
months early. You were furious to breathe. The EMT
allowed me to touch your head,
to feel the damp pulse of your life. Then you were
helicoptered away,
leaving me to that small-town hospital bed,
shade-less bulbs burning in the halls.   Child,

how was it for you last night,
your friends kissing behind the dune, the sea withdrawing,
consumed by its own story?
Did you feel it again? Your solitude, alien,
delectable as moonlight.

KAI-LILLY KARPMAN

Grover

I'm thinking of my mother's childhood dog
Grover, who was eaten alive by maggots
Half a mile from their farm.
He went into the Kansas wood.
Curled up alone. I imagine he saw moss hanging,
Heard squirrels chittering, wind
Only signaled by the leaves.
I hope it was loud there, louder than the sound
Of muscle churning, digested back into the wound.
After three of these days he still wasn't home,
So my mother's oldest brother Jeff went to look for him.
Jeff lifted Grover's tail and saw the swarm of
White maggots in his skin.
That dog didn't even try to bite him.
I don't know if dogs ever hope for a gun.
It is still the only time my mother saw Jeff cry.
I'm embarrassed to be so blue, to have briefly considered
Comparing life to the relentless mouth of a maggot.
It is August, and
I can still watch the sun turn the sides of the buildings pink
While an evening cathedral wears a peaceful face.
As God's placeholder, a child rides a scooter. A bookstore has a sale.
But listen World, I do not love you enough to forgive you.

Daisy Fried
Glorious Piner

I met Glorious Piner when she was just graduating from the University of the Arts in Philly. Her work was fresh then, and mature. Now she's finishing her MFA at the University of Maryland—and keeps so many balls in the air, it's breathtaking. She translates, she podcasts, she edits, and she writes in many modes. Always—as in these prose poems—her language is muscular, detailed, playful, also as serious as can be. Starting to read a Glorious Piner poem, I never know where I'll end up. She works the language for its multitude of possibilities, attentive to the life of the mind and heart as well as to trouble, danger, the life of the street. Read her to see an all new combination of styles—the journalistic, the lyric, the experimental—and be reminded how important it is to go deeper and farther, to feel more, to analyze more, to stay alert. Maybe to live more too.

DAISY FRIED

My Destination

after Rimbaud's "Le Dormeur du Val"

There's a green hollow where the river croons,
madly hanging silver rags on the grasses
hanging its glad rags on the grasses
and there's a museum crouching on the ridge
like a woman trying to unhunch her shoulders
after long difficulty. There's a river undulating,
a limb turning from a body, a silver river
trickling, not much rain of late. On the bike trail
I smashed my behemoth rental on purpose
into the foldable a man with padded shorts
dragged into my lane to show he needn't
notice rules. Unhurt by the impact, he vibrated
outrage at my audacity, he shivered
with umbrage derived from his abilities
picking stocks and inferiors, a tale
of his own deserving. I sped away and docked
my bike and my iPhone beeped confirmation.
In a room behind a room in a room of the museum
I arrived at my destination: two eyeholes bored
in rustic doors: the Duchamp peepshow *Étant Donné*—
Given—"a picture without a picture plane"—
"a surprise attack" by naked genitals. Supine
nude mannequin hand—all out of scale
as if she were Mona Lisa reaching
behind herself to scrabble in distant hills—
raises a trickling lantern, glimmering
lightfall. *Feet in the gladioli . . .*
Feet in wild violets . . . cresses . . . in chicory . . .
Nature, nurse her warm; she's cold. Frightening,
the gash hooked, hairless, between her legs,

44

question between her legs. *Berce-le* . . .
Lustrous, she's dead? Only sleeping?
I tried to move my eyes, I really did,
to see her face, this moved them
off the eyeholes, then I saw nothing.

NOTE: Italicized lines are my versions of lines from Rimbaud's "Le Dormeur du Val" ("The Sleeper in the Valley"), in which a young soldier appears merely to be sleeping. The phrases "a picture without a picture plane" and "a surprise attack" are from Pia Høy's article, "Marcel Duchamp—Étant donnés: Deconstructed Painting," trans. John Irons, from *tout-fait: The Marcel Duchamp Studies Online Journal.*

GLORIOUS PINER

A Portrait of a Chicken

Quite frankly, it portends nothing other than itself: a deflated, red cut-throat, a stiff, insouciant cock, cut and portioned inside the bad, bad slaughter-farm, rats still scurry around the slop-bucket; and disproportionate, its style, when sawed, is something like white or raw, like a weather-worn cutlet—what it means to sell hard—to sell something of war-copper, a paragon or parallax of ruin—a brick of sorts. Which had to have been why the D.E.A. agent wrote, when he wrote, "packed & sealed for distribution." But anyone could become a warrior for luxury and lure, or march through the lore and hook of its portentous buck and wing. Anyone could be totally dazed by it, the rouge ravenous claw, that funky, self-conscious shuck, that decaying groovy buck, that brown and caw that sounds, when steady enough, like the tenor of tin, or the clamorous song of the Sirens.

A Portrait of a Brick of Cocaine (1)

And still: not to part, but to oar—as herring gulls oar air & the ocean's white crest, wrestling with the wind splits the tar-feathered wings from the white supple breasts.

A Portrait of a Brick of Cocaine (2)

Almost inevitably, from the trap came a trapping—a stiff white, powder. Or, a wild, uncontainable power—a blackness the substance of cave walls, and their terrific captures: those charcoal stamps of loosed stock mules, in the rock, stampeding through a pasture.

A Portrait of the Word

In the beginning, there was the Word, and within a word are
many characters. This, surely, will frustrate any man of letters. He
will soon find that each word fosters—if Oriental—a vibrant and
unified community. Or—if Anglo-European—the melancholy
and mania of Undifferentiated Schizophrenia. *Word?* Word, son.
And every character has, at its core, a baseline—in layman's terms,
a faith, in secular terms, a safe-word. And from this baseline, the
cold and rigid limbs of a character reach beyond themselves, freeing
an eternal charge—like the Black that frees the starlight from the
star—or that binds the wings of the starling to the night. So, every
word rages against the sentence, every word is convict or conviction
—a word, then, is an attempt at grace, every word—wait for it, my
nigga—is a messiah.

Dan O'Brien
Ananda Lima

I admire this poem—as I admire Ananda Lima's work in general—for its grace. The shape of "delivery" evokes the restaurant worker on an urban street corner in a photograph by B.A. Van Size that serves as Lima's ekphrastic subject. This shape could just as easily represent a figure reaching to receive; what matters is this reaching, and the quotidian yet life-giving moments of connection.

There is grace also in the precision and seeming ease of these lines, the delicate groupings of word and phrase, a clarity of reading despite an absence of punctuation (excepting the question mark—itself a kind of typographical reaching). Lima implies here, and in much of her work, a critique of the inequities of a caste system that we wish to transcend, or at least to elude; "*parto*," the speaker reminds us, "is also a verb / *to leave*." The protagonist of this poem, however, is our server who, "hungry / like God", delivers our sustenance. This is a wistful poem. These strangers passing on the street are masked, their breathing necessarily screened, their giving and receiving—of goods, speech, love—impeded but still imperfectly occuring.

DAN O'BRIEN

Parents Crying

Did my father cry? Impossible to imagine. Only once I saw my mother
do it freely, childishly even—the night my brother leapt from a window
in our attic. She sobbed in my arms atop the attic stairs, instructing me:
"This is a secret we must take to our graves." There were many times
she'd been crying alone, hunched on the side of the marriage bed when
I'd just waltz right in—just like my daughter waltzes in as I write this;
and I knew like my daughter knows: my eyes are like my mother's—
raw, overfull, quivering. But we don't know why, my daughter and I,
do we? Are they divorcing? Does she wish she could? Is she mourning
a love affair, or its lack thereof? Is she reliving some radical
disfiguring (figurative or otherwise)? Does she remember her mother
locking her away in a broom closet overnight for crying too long and
too loudly? And how did my mother react, feeling found out like that
by her son? She dried up; flustered, as I am. Livid-proud. She denied by
pretending, as I pretend too. Why stain our children with our tears?
It's hard to say anyway which inflicts the most harm, revelation or
evasion. Yet in this way my mother made it clear: she did not want me
crying either. The louder I cried in the crib (I suspect) the farther away
she slipped. Like my wife losing her temper with me again a day or two
before the next chemo drip; or her inexplicable, understandable rage
now that treatment is over—hers and mine both, though her cancer
came first, overtaken by mine. But I digress: I never learned how to cry
correctly; my tears flow copiously, occasionally, but confusingly
because rarely do I cry about what saddens me, but rather in response
to countless inexhaustible obsessions concerning questions that can't be
controlled or resolved anyway. Recurrence. Marriage. And invariably
in the dawn light I'm mortified, having forgotten the hurt that inspired
such lunacy. I don't feel it, you see; I simply fail to feel it. Only writing
has ever helped me. As my mother seemed to imply as she handed me
the pen: *You cannot cry to me so cry to them.* Yet the louder I cry the farther
away some slip. Like those who skipped town the moment they heard
the word cancer. He'd driven through a midnight blizzard to collect me

from a bus stop in Rutland; I brought a bunch of perfumed magazines to her in the hospital after her appendix burst. I married them—actually emceed their wedding! Yet who am I to judge? When a second mother to my wife lay dying of a recurrence of ovarian, I could not bring myself to say goodbye. I feared I had to save my tears. My wife and I fought bitterly about that. Quiet as could be. In the night while our daughter dreamed. I hope she never wakes to hear us through the walls weeping for any reason; one of us lost, or both. An absence unending. I hope she never has cause to read these words. Our daughter cries well though, so far, it must be said in our defense: eye to eye, full-throated— she sings; then serene. Unburdened. Unblamed. Maybe it's not too late to learn from her.

ANANDA LIMA

delivery

On B.A. Van Sise (untitled photograph)
and Michelangelo (*The Creation of Adam*)

on the photograph I see   what I was
      not seeking   god in the outstretched arm
the reach the almost   touch I can almost
remember how it was   almost
      all of us   together
      in hunger   for each other
   parto is the noun   for *delivery*
     in portuguese   as in child
       not   pastrami sandwich
   at the center   of the frame almost turning
    the corner   I see her hungry
      like god   hungers for giving
  his languid creation   breath
    in her cloud?   halo?
      drapery   of stickers
       she   stretching
       he   masked in her likeness
      parto   is also a verb
     to leave   in the first person
       or   *to divide*
    god knows   what is like
   to be lonely   too

David Wojahn

Adam Grabowski

"Please Catalogue Your Items According to Their Value" is a wry and affectionate ode to how so many of us were initiated into the pleasures and wonders of reading (and writing) poetry. It praises the artistry of Jim Carroll, but it's also an account of how certain books, as they tatter and their spines break, become ever-more talismanic for us. There will never be an equivalence to this in the realm of the digital.

DAVID WOJAHN

In Memory of Hauro Nakajima

After his final Godzilla, he operates a bowling alley,
    his suit no longer weighing 200 pounds,
        no fiberglass patinaed with latex scales & nodes.

his arms & prehensile hands no longer anviling
    down upon the rooftops & commuter train trestles
        of a scale model Ginza. No buildings riven

pyrotechnically, like napalm firestorms induced
    by Yankee Superfortresses. No jump cuts
        to fleeing crowds as he hisses fire, snapping

fighter jets in half. Do not underestimate his artistry.
    He could walk 30 feet, whereas other suit-men
        could scarcely manage 10. & his lumber

was praised as "realistic," for he'd spent days
    studying the gait of an elephant named Indira.
        Hour after hour at the Ueno Park Zoo,

like Rilke scribbling notes beneath his panther's
    cramped art deco cage. Round eyes of hammered tin,
        painted yellow sclera, he could only see through

the open mouth, following a flashlight beam
    projected on the floor before him.
        But tonight it is 3 a.m. & he walks no longer

like a god, rinsing beer mugs, running a cloth
    along the gleaming zinc bar, then placing
        the upturned barstools there, dusting the pinball

& pachinko machines. 10,000 miles distant
    having lost his route on the Great Northern
        after 25 years, my father has retired to his woodshop,

to his flasks of Jim Beam, to cleaning the rifle
    he plans to cumbersomely point
        against his head or heart. No first act, nor a second,

no breathing of fire, only the wheeze
    of emphysema. Instead, he is the panther,
        ever-bewildered & pacing to oblivion his paralytic will.

Instead, he is Indira, a ball & chain upon the right
    rear leg, gangrenous beneath its steel clamp.
        Hauro Nakajima has almost finished closing up.

In his stocking feet, he shuffles down
    the polished alleys, resetting pins. Here,
        the ruins of a strike, there a 7 10 split.

ADAM GRABOWSKI

Please Catalogue Your Items
According to Their Value

for JC, and DW

I've decided—after last week's tropical depression—that my high school
    copy of Jim Carroll's *Fear of Dreaming*,
scuffed as it is (& stained & sun-bleached & Scotch-taped together) is
    the only book I'd brave a tornado for
though the windows they bend & my family howls at my back. This
    decision has nothing to do
with Jim's quick-Sharpie'd signature, & there's nothing pressed between
    the pages worth a damn, either—no
rose petals, no wedding favors to keep holy—I broke the centerpiece—I
    sneezed my way right out of the garden—really
such determination wouldn't have anything to do with anything save
    the fact that
this is the book I've held onto the longest &—like my wedding ring,
    or the St. Christopher's Medal
I've got stuck to the dashboard of my car—I've grown wary of what
    happens once it's gone.
Probably nothing, but I'm not taking any chances. Not right now.
Not with all this weather.

Elena Karina Byrne
Cathy Colman

Cathy Colman's poetic genius resides in her sleight-of-hand ability to juxtapose the angst-ordinary with the transcendent extraordinary while recreating our fragile world anew. Her lyrical poem "The Fear Circus" instigates that universal feeling of surprise while striking at the heart of her personal relationship with her dead parents. The visually cinematic, musically bound lines simultaneously delight and horrify, both "both mud-sick & / gold-unrequited"—all the while, as each descending line creates that "thrilling vertigo" one has when confronting Time's absence. After all, she says, "It forgets about itself" in the unique way we cannot. A perfect, allegorical poem with a circular structure can also be read backward as read forward, experienced inside the dream room, or on the ledge-precipice of reality. Full of unease and longing, those entangled energies defy denouement. Yet, measure for measure, this poem seamlessly unravels a rhythmed narrative that catches our breath in its trapeze net's "apron." I can't get enough of her work. Read any of her three books and you'll agree.

ELENA KARINA BYRNE

Dalí's Gluton Recipe Dead: Politics

*Rest assured that for each member you will pull off he will
scream so that he will be eaten live rather than dead.*

Nearly asleep in sweet trifling she lay out alone on this NYC lawn, raw
dirty pigeons skirting a circle edge's raked flame of leaves. Who
walks past
her served-up bathing body with burgundy sun on the way to work
doesn't
see the fountain's web-footed waters, its spring horses flash & stir,
its escape
of water, loose silver chains spit breaking onto the concrete. Didn't
see the corn
flour cakes walking to school, the jellied cod or siren shoulder. *Pierced
heart &*
Prawnparfait daily hurry on their way, their way. *Le Chat flanqué* de
Rats from
these streets cut chatter for another's scent, pass salt under their tails.
How many
Guineafowl for a murder, pig skin, headless eels peppered on bread
today? Before
night's rolling-pin arrives, before cicadas start their singing-out the
heat, he drops
feet from her, a Peregrine & his pigeon flesh strips of bacon, carrots
& onion soaked
in cherries. She pays no notice, her little bits of butter clarified swim-
suit orange peel
& roe set onto the middle sour grass since all sounds of the fountain
are salpicon.
We the people, we *ought to transform the art of eating into an
olographic ecstasy!*

CATHY COLMAN

The Fear Circus

I teeter on the tightrope between my mother's death
& my father's last words. Mother flew up & came
　　apart, all naked petals & pearly-footed.

Father fell down into the cow patch of black & white
TV, the once virgin land pocked with bright noise.
I miss them like the Ring Toss misses its rings,
　　like a jar misses its pennies, both mud-sick &

gold-unrequited. Inside, the empty jar always
there, counting to itself, zero equals zero
equals zero equals the Quetzal-feathered serpent
　　with his twin, Xoloti, the dog-headed god

that guides the dead. It was not in my act to murder
them, my parents, even though I remember screaming,
"I wish you were dead!" & my father thought back,
"I wish you were never born." Mother said,
　　"I wish you were always being born."

It's difficult on the rope because it gives me a thrilling
vertigo that comes right before suicide, its physics like
the ancient debate between the Big Bang & intelligent
　　design. Time is absent. It forgets about itself.

Even though my mother's romance wants
The Strongman to catch me. I've always been
my father's contortionist, able to make love to
myself, picking up dimes with my toes & throwing
　　them into the open mouths of the crowd.

Flávia Rocha

Ruy Ventura

Ruy Ventura builds spaces for cohabitation of polyphonic existences. The poet's voices—as in the best Portuguese tradition (think of Fernando Pessoa's heteronymous and Raul Brandão's poetic assessment of villagers, for example)—are also very cohesive in the sense that they share a range of interests and a purposely recurrent vocabulary (as in Brandão) that expands at every turn. They read and feel like flexions of an internal poetic quest—one that is intensely philosophical, aesthetic and lyrical. The construction is precise and the language bends toward metaphorical insight. This is what Ventura does in two of his recent books, *Detergente* (2016) and *Contramina* (2012). *Detergente* is almost structured as a play, as a conversation between two characters, while *Contramina* contains a series of prose poems presented in the form of a dialogue among dozens of well-known and lesser-known real or fictional characters, all of which are called only by their first names. The cast of characters is broad and deceptively random, running from biblical figures, such as John, the evangelist, to Edward Degas, to Virginia Wolf's character Orlando. . . Under these sets of names, permissively (sometimes the same name refers to more than one character), Ventura creates a kind of mirror effect, in which the characters trigger and complete each other's thoughts to compose, ultimately, the poet's own poetic fabric.

Ventura is a well established poet and editor in the Portuguese literary scene, but, like many contemporary poets from countries and languages that are less represented in translation, he is somewhat new to the American public. As a Brazilian poet who has lived in the U.S. for several years and has recently landed in Lisbon, I'm eager to meet poets who I share a language with. Not only a syntax, but also a way of approaching language in poetry. I'm happy I ran into Ruy Ventura's poetical spaces, which seem to operate outside of time, as they may fit, always at ease in their complex structures.

FLÁVIA ROCHA

Contra todas as expectativas

Contra todas as expectativas
nos esforçamos. Nos humanos
o instinto animal é o mais racional.
Somos muitos a farejar
a materialidade inconcebível
sobre a qual futuros se constróem :
    suspensos nos andaimes oxidados
    do presente, às vezes nos fazemos ouvir.
Martelamos o óbvio em estacas de acrílico
e de longe o imbróglio brilha no ar :
    atônito, vibrante
    objetivo, extraordinário.
Nossa rebeldia salva algumas vidas
na base, o resto
somos obrigados a negociar.

FLÁVIA ROCHA

Against all expectations

> Against all expectations
> we make an effort. In humans
> the animal instinct is the most rational.
> We are many to sniff out
> the unconceivable materiality
> upon which futures are built :
> > suspended in the oxidized scaffoldings
> > of the present, sometimes we make ourselves heard.
> We hammer the obvious into acrylic stakes
> and from afar the imbroglio sparkles in the air :
> > astonishing, vibrant
> > objective, extraordinary.
> Our rebellion saves a few lives
> on the base, the rest
> we're forced to negotiate.

An excerpt from a book-length poem titled *Exosfera*, which was released simul-
taneously in Portugal and in Brazil in 2021 by Editora Nós. Translated from the
original in Portuguese by the author.

RUY VENTURA

Agostinho

uma figura atravessa a imperfeição da luz talvez, perdendo-
se, encontre o rumo que conduz do joio ao indizível. pode
forçar a nuvem, sabendo de antemão—a nuvem permanece.
ou criar outra nuvem e esclarecer a sequência dos veios da
madeira. nela terá de entrar, contudo, um líquido escuro.
talvez assim a espiral governe (mantenha em movimento) o
motor que comove a existência.

João

a velocidade auxilia a limpeza do motor. a incerteza do
asfalto configura nos circuitos todas as sinapses que a sombra
edifica. o voo não é, contudo, suficiente para limpar do
habitáculo todas as marcas de ferrugem deixadas pelo sal e
pela água. a oxidação toma conta das entranhas e lança no
estômago sedimentos e limalhas que o trânsito não consegue
eliminar. mesmo limpo, o motor não ignora a entrada da erva
pelas fendas do metal. chuva e calor mancham, rebentam, a
chapa (e a memória). o motor sobrevive ao concurso da
existência. sem velocidade, sobrevive—diluído no ácido
das esferas.

RUY VENTURA translated by FLÁVIA ROCHA

Augustin

a figure crosses the imperfection of light. perhaps, losing itself, it will find the path that leads from weed to the unspeakable. it can force the cloud, knowing from the start— the cloud remains. or create another cloud and clarify the sequence of grains in the wood. there, though, a dark liquid must go in. perhaps this way the spiral will govern (sustaining its movement) the engine that drives existence.

John

speed helps to clean the engine. the certainty of asphalt configures in its circuits all the synapsis the shadow engineers. though this flight isn't sufficient to erase from the interior all the rust marks left by salt and water. oxidation takes over the entrails and lays into the stomach sediments and filings it's unable to eliminate in its transit. even clean, the engine doesn't ignore the grass entering through cracks in the metal. rain and heat stain, break, the slab (and memory). the engine survives the concourse of existence. it survives without speed—diluted in acid from the spheres.

An except from the collection *Contramina* (Editora Licorne, 2012). It references, simultaneously, Augustin of Hippo, philosopher/Agostinho da Cruz, poet/ Agostinho da Silva, philosopher, and John the Evangelist/John of the Cross, poet. Translated from the original in Portuguese by Flávia Rocha.

Garrett Hongo

Alycia Pirmohamed

Alycia Pirmohamed is an intensely lyrical young poet of South Asian descent and Canadian nationality who, nearly a decade ago, was sent to study with me by her mentor Derek Walcott. Her poetry introduces a sensuous heteroglossia that fractures common language usages with numerous lexical crossings that explode expectation with fresh potentials of the said and new portents of the unsaid, creating unexpected conjunctions of meaning that release undercurrents of passion leveraging language out of the banal into the thrilling. In "Midnight vessel across the great sea," her heightened awareness of synechdochal relations develops chains of metaphoricity that transmogrify *moon* to *window* to *stone breaking the skin, body* to *echo of iambs* to *ancestral threads, drool* to *heirloom hair* to *reeds* [of migration] that part the *velvet* petals that *bloom* on the *volta* of her lover. Her poem asks us to follow the creases and interstices of meaning, to run a finger across the raised repairs and golden grout of *kintsugi* across the surfaces of her strophes, her language of new rootedness and stitchery threading through her lyric consciousness so that it is travel that constitutes itself as identity rather than origin, yearning that asserts itself as purport and the truer experience over mere requital.

GARRETT HONGO

Reading Miguel Hernández in Bert Meyers' Library

A room surrounded by wooden bookshelves, slim volumes of poetry
                                    with colorful spines,
an arcana not only of knowledge, but of human acts on stages
        both everyday and unimaginable:
                        peasants planting corn in rows of dry earth,
a prisoner being buried whose poems were scratched in blood
                                    on his own clothes,
a fisherman who sings to his nets as he sets them out in patches
                                    on a shallow sea,
a sybarite sauntering through a Parisian park, scorning the bronze Rodins,
a mother grieving at the impassive gates of tyranny, her son
                                    disappeared by police.

I learned reverence for the quiet actions of the mind,
                those who inscribed precise, passionate words
            onto the chambers of remembrance within languages,
brogues and patois, creoles and chimeras of speech, rhythmic jungles
                    traversed by the resolute beasts of peace.

I read Miguel, Aimé, Sappho, Nazim, Anna and Renato.
                            .   I ate of earth, drank of ice,
saw with eyes tutored by weeping, my body swayed to the cycling music
                                    of eternities.
I read to arrive as my teacher saw me, cleansed of cares, swollen heart
                    ready to mourn, tuned to the old music.

ALYCIA PIRMOHAMED

Midnight vessel across the great sea

What kind of river, then, has no middle?

—Édouard Glissant

Another bloom after the first bloom   inheritance is a form
of second sight   in the past someone with my birthmarks
predicted the next moon   the upheaval   my own ebb.
My body is the echo of her iambs   a tradition that sieves
right through   my ancestor's thread.   I am slick with
rosewater and cat's eye   —I can't choose between
survival or pleasure.   In the past   someone who looked
like me fell   into the valley of roses   five times a day.
This echo is   another velvet petal   submerged in the drool
of my mouth   I am submerged   in the drool of her mouth.
My second sight is an heirloom   a volume of sonnets
passed down   a line of flight   as if she is more image
than intent   more midnight than syllable   the eye before
the eye   the root beneath my poem.   I am a remembrance
and she is my volta—   an echo blooms   this echo is her hair
parting into my hair   she is the fine dark strand   across
my memory   she glides like a reed   a silhouette of green
across the great sea   her poetry strikes through   my window
like a stone   breaking the skin   memory of water.

Gerry LaFemina
Madeleine Barnes

I've known Madeleine Barnes since she was an undergraduate at Carnegie Mellon, and for the last several years she's been one of the co-curators with Lynn McGee and myself of the Lunar Walk reading series. Madeleine is an amazing literary citizen, working with journals and promoting other writers.

As much as she shines in her service to other writers, she shines on the page. Her first book, *You Do Not Have to Be Good*, demonstrates her range as a poet, moving between meditative lyrics, more narrative poems, and more experimental/fractal work, but always with the same mix of pathos and rigorous artistry. These are poems that invite the reading into their central dramas, that invite us to become part of the experience, and invite the poem to become part of our experience.

"Memory Constellation" captures the way images of events make and inform memory. As with any constellation: all we see are the stars, the key images: the cigarettes, the letters, the yearbooks. But the whole picture is what we have to imagine the lines that make a fuller drawing, that brings to life the myth. And isn't our childhood a kind of myth? Reading this poem, I think of the great Jerry Stern quote (another Pittsburgh poet) ". . . what we call nostalgia is for the life we didn't live." This nebulous space between what actually happened and how we remember it, becomes the reality for the reader. Toward the end, she says, "Some people say we won't find meaning / in this life" reminding us of that we read poems to help us find meaning, they become the myths we use to understand our world.

GERRY LA FEMINA

Post-Valentine

Twenty days into February, the only flowers funereal
blooms on sheared stems, arranged for aesthetics. Isn't this
the way—finding beauty in what's dying? The goth kids
thought so, back in the day, with their black eyeliner, dyed
hair, Bauhaus on the turntable. Dark aesthetes. Thus,
the mortician works, part surgeon, part beautician
with her make up case, her cat gut, her photos,
her astonishing bonesaw laughter at the table. Such a strange
blind date, all her tales about the living & nearly departed.
She said what shade she'd blush my cheeks, asked
if I wanted to be viewed wearing spectacles. What would I need
to see at that point? Don't ask what year this was.
I recall only that it'd been the coldest winter in memory:
winds unfurled like surprised birds, the kind
so startling & vibrant that you'd stop breathless right there.
A wind like that. A cold like that. Street lights
laid haloes on the ice as we walked, & I thought
I wouldn't sleep with her or even kiss her goodnight.
There were few people out; their cars huddled close to the curb.
Some dark wave band—maybe Sisters of Mercy—
on the radio. Despite my intentions, I went upstairs
when invited for coffee & felt an undertow of disappointment
as her pager buzzed, & she had to go to work. Someone,
no doubt, had died. Happens all the time. She kissed me
before leaving, teeth pressed for a moment against my mouth,
not sensuous or sexy, just her small, sharp bicuspids.
They sew the mouth of the dead shut, let the living speak.
She said she never wore black anymore, so cliche;
said I resembled a buzzard in my long coat, such a handsome,
homely bird. Her jacket was cardinal red, lipstick bright

in the deep night. Then gone. Just wind. I'd almost forgotten
such brilliance existed. Because snow absorbs sound,
the streets seemed quieter, or maybe it was my solitude.
In the window displays all the hearts & cupids had been
replaced by green shamrocks & leprechauns ready
to celebrate the saint who'd banished snakes from the land.

MADELEINE BARNES

Memory Constellation

Pittsburgh, hometown, childhood,
compass that speaks, center of gravity
that holds everything together: shelter,
storm, axis—in my childhood bedroom
are the cigarettes smoked with a friend
who is no longer alive, letters
from my fifth-grade librarian,
& yearbooks full of signatures I can't identify.
As a kid, I could find meaning in anything.
I lived in the space between longing & magic,
imagination unfolding in countless direction,
picking up branches & nesting fibers.
There was always something I wanted to make.
Teachers tried to prepare us for harms
we could barely envision: cyclones, bomb threats,
shootings—we walked into windowless hallways,
knelt, & covered our heads. They gave us maps
& circled the exits. Should I have paid better attention?
We laughed when we shouldn't have laughed,
whispered through drills & assemblies.
I remember moments of stillness
interrupted by the sound of life-flight helicopters
& the science teacher who taught us about
the Doppler effect. She told me that she knew
I would be *saved*. These pieces of life—
who will save them? All I want
is to know that what we find in this world
will somehow be conserved.
I leave the addresses of the dead in my family
untouched, but who will save mine?
It's as if they still live there. I believe they do.

I walk into my mother's garden
& it has grown. I try to constellate
my memories of pollen,
the aroma I associate with truth.
Do you remember every garden?
Some people say we won't find meaning
in this life. They say everything will vanish & dissolve,
that we have no home on this earth.
Fireflies, rivers, graduation, someone playing the piano, violets—
they say we weren't designed to remember all of it.
Despite time, my most reliable hiding place,
I've never been one of them.

Gregory Orr
Safiya Sinclair

So many of Safiya Sinclair's poems make me think of Emily Dickinson's invitation-as-challenge: "Dare you see a Soul at the *White Heat*? / Then crouch within the door...." (#365) Sinclair's poems often draw us within the door of her poems so near an event or experience that language is twisted by the heat of that heart-forge where meanings are made, where imagination fuses discrete things into that single, sinuous and sonorous intensity a lyric can become. Present in "Mirabilia" are self and sibling as children clustered around a glass jar containing a thrashing and venomous giant centipede—the intensity of their engagement melds them ("our heads / one nested dread, observing // the predator gone dark / with our wanting"). Parents ghosting the background, but the central intensity of the speaker is so focused she *partakes* of that creature's being as the poem itself writhes and thrashes down the page. Sinclair has a way of singing herself to the under-sense of things—where things mingle and meld. She's fastened to things by *fascination* (whose root is *witchcraft*)—where the intensity of her involvement forces them to release not only their own secrets but those of the speaker. How laughably and laudably different from that distanced and fearful stance D. H. Lawrence takes in "Snake," his own encounter with the dangerous, creaturely other.

GREGORY ORR

Some of us, when we're young

Some of us, when we're young,
Can't get enough of poems
About sex and death—

We're convinced they'll instruct
Us what to expect when
Those two mysteries finally arrive.

No one tells us even the best maps
Often just guess what's next.

No one says: "Old mysteries are
Always new
When they finally happen to you."

She unbuttons her cotton blouse;
The car coming toward you
Begins its slow slide
Across the black ice.

There you are.

To warn or advise—equally useless.

SAFIYA SINCLAIR

Mirabilia

noun (plural)
marvels; miracles.

Suddenly we were all together again,
my siblings and I, coiled there

moon after moon, watching
a brooding centipede

thrash its shell-and-serpentine
whip against the jarred glass.

Every bright four o'clock
bloomed its old news

then shrunk back into
its petals, just as we had learned

to fear our father's shadow.
We did not expect it—

the creature's gasp erupting,
hissing frantic, our hardened

thoughts stuck in its gathering blue of
agonies. Then that sour garden

of childhood, another afternoon
we had long thought hidden,

now pulled up, grown thick
and burst like a cut-lip,

cherries we were forbidden
but gorged down anyway

until they made us sick. The
pure emptying feast of it.

Here everything nursed everything
else back to its nature;

small children of a mercy
we never knew. How it railed—

claw-legged and quick,
prehistoric hunger arching pincers

toward our cruelty, our heads
one nested dread, observing

the predator gone dark
with our wanting,

knowing too well its lethal
need to escape, only aching

to destroy any vulnerable thing.
The way we'd held our mother

underwater, and the way we had
been taught to. I should have

given myself to it—
drowned heavy and visionary

with its poison, worn its rakes
and hundred-legs as sails down my back—

but instead I walked myself
a hound inside its hunger, caught

a neon lizard in my palms
but did not crush it, placed it tender

and alive into the hot jar instead, where the
centipede moved as nature

taught it to move—alien blade upon
the lizard-skull, spiked pincers

singing, an acid bell, the lizard's squeak
dissolving its own rattle, our fangs

on fire, jaw-struck, tooth-struck,
a scythe of slow skin boiled down

to bone and spine, to tail, until
there was nothing left. The lizard stripped

sightless, skeletal, gone with our numb
marvel at what this day had lathed

of us—razor-dark, divine, our blood
still brimming its madcap halo,

children of a sun
born devouring

its own back.

Jane Hirshfield
Danusha Laméris

It was difficult to choose a single poem from the group Danusha Laméris sent when I invited her to join me in *Plume*'s tenth anthology. Each of the poems carried the strengths I've come to expect in Laméris's work—the sure arc of genuine exploration and genuine feeling, wide-awake language, a capacious world of reference, the music and syntax that mark thought that takes place in body as well as in mind. Her poems hold the tension of actual work being done by their own writing. They've thrilled me since I first discovered a small set in a journal and looked again: "Who is this?" I commend to you her two published books. They answer that question, and then answer further, bringing fresh news of who you yourself are, and of word, of world.

I chose in the end a poem that raises a physical response each time I read it. It was only after I went to look for a poem of my own to accompany hers that I even remembered that I have a poem, written thirty years ago now, with a similar title, or remembered my own subsequent book of "heart" poems, *The Lives of the Heart*. Danusha Laméris's poem: "They Say the Heart Wants." Mine; "What the Heart Wants."

The two poems reflect what feels already different eras of world, outer and inner. I don't think I could now, for instance, write a poem holding an image of an elephant in domesticated circumstances, even though the image is metaphor, even though the tension between the animal's actual power, strength, dignity, and capacities and its kneeling before what is asked is the poem's very point. I find the thought now too painful for use in a poem. Yet the side-by-side placing of these two poems feels to me worth offering here, as specimen likenesses. Both poems take for their opening premise a common-enough phrase, one that has also a history. Emily Dickinson wrote in letter #262, to Mary Bowles: "The Heart wants what it wants—or else it does not care—" In different phrasing, there is the famous aphorism of the seventeenth-century logician and theologian, Blaise Pascal: "The heart has its reasons, of which the reason knows nothing." The heart-wanting's shifting appears in a ninth-century tanka by Ono no Komachi: "How invisibly / it changes color / in this world, / the flower / of the human heart." Nahuatl poems from Mesoamerica and ancient Sumerian proverbs hold also this feeling and changing heart.

My own poem was written from inside the throes of heart-want. Danusha Laméris considers the phrase with greater perspective, from further away. She questions the phrase, turns it, bicycles off, goes visiting, ponders. The seed of strong emotion is slipped in at first casually, halfway through a long list. But by her poem's end, that tucked-in seed returns full-grown, revealed. And each time I reach those final lines, I feel myself, along with the author, physically shaken by longing's remembrance. As Sappho, in seventh century BCE, near the start of the Western poetic tradition, once was shaken: "Eros shook my heart, like strong mountain winds storming an oak."

JANE HIRSHFIELD

What the Heart Wants

See then
what the heart wants,
that pliable iron
sprung to the poppy's redness,
the honey's gold, winged
as the heron-lit water is:
by reflecting.
As an aged elephant answers
the slightest, first gesture of hand,
it puts itself at the mercy—
utterly docile, the forces
that brought it there vanished,
fold into fold.
And the old-ice ivory, the unstartlable
black of the eye that has travelled so far
with the fringed, peripheral howdah
swaying behind, look mildly back
as it swings the whole bulk of the body
close to the ground. Over and over
it does this, bends to what asks.
Whatever asks, heart kneels and offers to bear.

First appeared in *The October Palace*, NY: HarperCollins, 1994.

DANUSHA LAMÉRIS

They Say the Heart Wants

what it wants, but no one tells you what it gets.
So here's a list, mine: tall grasses, blowing in the wind,

swirled glass cups, peacock blue, bought in Lebanon.
Fog off the California cliffs, dark boulders on the shore.

Billie Holiday's *I'll be seeing you in all the old
familiar places*, cycling through my auditory cortex.

Dogs pulling at the leash. Small white plates
of wild greens and beets. The time a man kissed

my hand when we met, then pressed my palm
to his cheek. Sei Shōnagon's eleventh-century list

of Things That Give One a Clean Feeling: *an earthen cup,
a new metal bowl, a rush mat, the play of light on water*

as one pours it into a vessel, a new wooden chest.
To which I add a drawer of beeswax candles,

steam rising from a pot of tea. So much stored
in the heart's farthest chambers. And even though

he's been dead for decades now, I still feel the kiss.
My whole arm shivers with its half-life.

Jeffrey Skinner

Ann Townsend

Ann Townsend's work is subtle, and this may be why she is not more visible. She takes her time with each collection of her poems, putting more years between the publication of each than is usual. The result is that each of her books is a complete experience—each poem exquisitely made, and placed in such thoughtful order the power of the whole is magnified.

To read her poems is to experience a chain of soft explosions. "A Sign" is a good example, I think. It is a love poem that begins *in media res*, with the lover focused on a blister on the speaker's palm, which he "set his tongue against . . ." Note the capture of physical gesture presented by the first line, the drama of its delay and completion through enjambment. And the connotative scope of the word *stigmata*, cast as straightforward and slightly comic response to the lover's action. Then, the lover's character, revealed by the following two couplets: the pretension and condescension of his generalizing statement about *all men*, quoting an ancient Greek poet—taking time out from an intimate moment to (*re?*) establish his scholarly creds. In a sly, satiric move, Ann casts her own poem in couplets, which Theognis used almost exclusively in his poems.

At the ending, in response to the lover's near banal quotation, we are given, "But a mouth is just a hive outwelling its sweetness, its sting." What a line! What a combination of particularized (opposed to the lover's generalities) mystery and ambiguity! And then: "Beauty dies, I said," a close that could be taken as weary rebuke, despite its truth, and the echo within it of a thousand previous poems and poets. A whole love story, a novel, within ten-lines, its complex dynamics ensnaring past as well as present. And the synecdoche at the center: a lover's wound, which the other uses, in the end, for his own purposes. Ann Townsend's poems are suffused by poetic grace, with a surface clarity that delivers the mystery directly to heart and mind.

JEFFREY SKINNER

Language of the Fall

Don't get the idea gentle
Is all, or most, or part of nature.
Maybe leaves got together
And decided on a calm drop;

But I think not. Wind
Shook the trees and leaves
Strafed down like words in flames,
Red-yellow-red-curses.

What's left are orations
On the forest floor.
Sometimes, wind's not gentle.
All are driven to earth.

ANN TOWNSEND

A Sign

He caught breath at the sight of the blood
blister on my palm, flayed, tender,

then set his tongue against it.
Excuse me, that's my stigmata, I said.

All men reach out to know, he said,
testing, probing for pain.

Besides, he said, Theognis knew
A beautiful thing inspires attachment.

But a mouth is just a hive outwelling
Its sweetness, its sting, I said. Beauty dies, I said.

Jennifer Franklin
Michelle Whittaker

Michelle Whittaker's unflinching eye invites her readers to consider a photograph of the speaker's pregnant, "unsmiling" mother twenty-six years ago in Kingston, Jamaica, in a time of political violence. Whittaker's work often considers what can be seen as well as what might be happening outside the moment of the poem—what is uncertain or unknowable—always aware that we can never fully know, through language, what another person experiences. Decades later in New York, the speaker considers arugula that has "gone to seed" and crossed the police barricade. Time and geography have not diminished human violence. The promise of escape through the door with the burning keyhole, to get to the American dream, may be as ephemeral as a cloud passing through the sky. But in the poem, the photograph of the mother holds such promise that it might be enough for us to hope for a better world that we might yet create. Of Michelle Whittaker's debut collection, *Surge*, Terrance Hayes writes, "Warmth and compassion power this amazing debut." Empathy pervades this luminous poem from her second manuscript.

JENNIFER FRANKLIN

Memento Mori: Mentor with Late-Stage Lewy Body Dementia

for Richard Howard (1929–2022)

The greatest mind I ever met now sits stiff
in a rented wheelchair. His hands seem to sew
invisible thread as his husband and I talk on a bench
in his courtyard. Like his beloved Penelope, weaving
endlessly on her loom only to pull her work apart each night,
he sits in turn patient and perturbed by something
we cannot see. He looks up at me only twice,
both times disappointed I am not someone else.

Across the courtyard, hydrangeas bloom,
oblivious and blue. His bent fingers grasp the hem
of my dress he once would have loved. I want him
to talk about his paused translation. I want to sit
next to him on his small sofa as he reaches for a book—
for him to mark these lines with his sharp black pen.

MICHELLE WHITTAKER

In Preparation for Ascendance

Consider Kingston, Jamaica, 1976.
Notice in the photo how your mother
in a mini skirt, body spiking as a Royal palm,
is three months pregnant & not smiling.

Notice where she looks for protection, as if
refocusing the exposure into a restraint
while a few miles away, political parties riot
with their flintlock triggers & ratchet knives,
as police round up & decimate the Trench Town.

Now consider being shown how the arugula
has gone to seed, in front of your New York
rental decades later, note how their heads
have crossed the broken police barricade.

Then look again at your beautiful mother
squinting beyond the frame at plumes rising
toward a nimbus cloud shaped like the United States.

See how the keyhole burns?

Jim Daniels

Julie Heming

"Derealization" is a poem from Julie Heming's honors thesis manuscript that she wrote at Carnegie Mellon University. Julie is a Korean-American adoptee born in Ilsan, South Korea. Her thesis explores her complex background growing up in a white family in Pennsylvania as she tries to figure out her own identity. Her tight, understated poems have a beautiful delicacy and a deceptive toughness as they deal with complex emotional issues. She knows just where to end her poems, which is a skill that will serve her well in the future. For such a young poet, she has a strong sense of craft. For example, in this poem, look at how she returns to the ghost and angel images at the end. Beautiful.

JIM DANIELS

Dinner at Lynn and Linda's with Ken and Jack

> Watch the International Space Station pass overhead from several thousand worldwide locations. It is the third brightest object in the sky and easy to spot if you know when to look up.

Dinner tonight with two married gay couples
and their kids. The women have a boy.
The men have a girl. Off playing
video games in the basement.

•

Growing up in Detroit, our imaginations
limited by polluted night sky, oblivious
to constellations of shame, we teased
each other for admiring the moon.
I never looked both ways
before I crossed the street.

•

Linda looks it up on her phone.
Lynn rolls her eyes. Still, we step out
onto the porch at 8:17 in Pittsburgh,
on October 23, and wait. We have not
turned our furnaces on, any of us,
but we will soon. Couples lean
into each other for balance
on this dizzy planet.

•

Linda serves tamarinds. None of us
have tried them before. For dessert,
we eat donuts decorated with dulled
vampire teeth and blurry witches—
who can make anything graceful

on a donut? They're made to be gripped
with certainty and bit into and swallowed.
We discuss donuts and memories
of donuts and Halloween and costumes
we no longer wear forever.

•

The kids stay inside. No interest
in seeing bright light zipper silent
across the sky, but the rest of us wait,
as we have waited for many things.
Porch light off, so as not to interfere,
yet tonight, we have found our way home.

•

After it passes, we go back in to round up
the kids, deal with life on earth.
The girl asleep in a father's arms, the boy lost
in the safe couch of home's dreamland.

•

Outside, we said nothing,
then we said *wow*—even that
too much in that grand silence
of changing seasons. Does the crew
circling the earth ever tire of wonder?

Ken's from Michigan, like me
with the flat vowels. Jack
was my student thirty years ago,
engaged to marry a girl.

Linda, my wife's oldest
and best friend. Linda and Lynn.
The Linns. What made her think
to watch the Space Station pass?

A white dot moving across the sky,
not a falling star, or a star at all.
I guess the kids take it for granted
what we can do now, the sky seamless,
not falling.

JULIE HEMING

Derealization

I left my body in Barnes & Noble,
sandwiched between the K's and the N's.

It's called derealization. I call it
digging my nails into my palms
to slide back into my skin,
or sometimes, a visitation,
to check in on you, birth mother,
and the life I was one sesame seed
away from living.

I perch outside your apartment
window in Ilsan, watching
your black hair fall into your face.

I want you to see me hanging
out on your ledge in a shift of white,
hand almost pressed against the glass.
I can't decide if I want to be a ghost
or an angel, what to do in this space
where we are neither here nor there.
You are mother but not.
I am Korean but not.

Snow begins to fall. My feet turn numb,
my nails dig harder into my skin.

By the time I am back to myself,
warm inside book-soaked light,
walking towards the magazines,
you finally look up.

But you've missed
both me and the snow.
When you look out your window,
all you see is melted flakes
like wing dust,
ghost breath.

Juan Felipe Herrera

J.J. Hernandez

Here, a talk, "broken" advise, a sermon to "Albert," by a "small town kid with a cyst in his brain," a denuncia, a fiery speaker denouncing the Maranatha, his "chant" says, that is the coming of the Lord. All is "absurd," all is reflexive analysis, a film, an accusation, a preparation " for the end of "civilization," the lurking of the "white man." There is violence and there is the will to "survive the apocalypse" with violence and the negation of the arrival of a future deity. And there are accidents and a serpent head severed with a "flathead shovel." There is no evil, there no gods — just this kid in an "apartment complex," this voice in this poem-apartment. A poem of fractal rooms. Here, a "concussion" of the sacred versus the profane, and another jittery pair, a loud "small town" speaker and a silent "Albert," perhaps the rage of existences without exit or entry, the "absurd."

JUAN FELIPE HERRERA

Son Borne of the Street Song

—inspired by the life of Gustav Mahler & his last Symphony no. 9

in the darkness,
in the exile—there is a sigh, a number 9
there is a son borne of the street song, the injured tympani red drum
there is a town *Jihlava*, a make-shift theatre &
rough-cut street dancers, there is a sky that welcomes him
his furious strings tasking the universe, his weaving of all things

the piccolo & the flute
oboes of furies tiny streams of burning slow breath
we wait in silence & face up
we notice the heavens, the turbulence &
wild sharp strokes & pieces of banned color & banned voices
their outcast Jewish hymn takes us to the endless seas

unknown choruses unknown winds & collapsing worlds
we enter we follow we enter we halt we are halted
vanishing harmonies you walk through quadrants of space
music what is it one note encompasses everything
one oboe returns why
your life beginning your life almost ending then ending
what do you hear in this vastness this movement before you
unknown forces whirl violins & the dead
the director's arms & hands sway shaking point dissolve
only still we stand now we only
left alone only Gustav Mahler lives on

by this bed this night this day this last cycle
falls into an ever returning descent of light
a voice a voice do you hear it hear it

J.J. HERNANDEZ

Small Town Kid Gets Jumped in an Apartment Complex in Fresno

A broken wrist, concussion, and possible cyst in his brain.
I guess I don't understand violence anymore. And yes,
It's a war out there. And yes, if you swing at me,
I'm going to swing back. Isn't that absurd, Albert?
This poem reads like some Tarantino bullshit with racist
diatribes about violence, like that scene in *Kill Bill: Volume 1*
where blood sprays onto the sunken dance floor, but I do prepare
for the race war. I do prepare for the end of civilization by listening
to chanting and metal, daring Him to end it.
Speak to me in the tongues of men and angels.
The white man will take my jobs if I let Him. Presence
is more important than safety. They know that. They
know with their serpent flags and rifles. Isn't Satan a serpent? Remember
He slithered up to Eve in the garden for fun. Was he offering
fruit or bullets? God in all His majesty said *the violent take by force.* It's
    absurd, I know.
I will survive the apocalypse, though, because I've killed a charging
rooster with a metal pipe like some *Jurassic Park* shit, & I know the
    mountains
taught me more than I think. I will not back down. I've cut a snake's head
off with a flathead shovel, just after it struck my shoe. Venom is absurd.
Pain is irrelevant. Maranatha, maranatha, I dare you. I'll be here waiting.

Kelli Russell Agodon

Katerina Canyon

Sometime in 2020 in the middle of the pandemic, poet Katerina Canyon reached out to me to ask if I wanted to read for her Zoom reading series "Canyon Poets." I arrived to be welcomed by a smart, vivacious, beautiful community of poets. There I saw Katerina's passion for poetry as well as her desire to make sure everyone's voice is heard. What I loved about Katerina is how well she listens and how there is always space and time for all—with Katerina, you are seen.

There is so much I admire about Katerina from how much she does for the community to her new book, *Surviving Home*, which transforms pain into poetry as it explores one woman's story of Black heritage and upbringing in America and challenges the beliefs of family and the fantasies of tradition.

Katerina is a voice that needs to be heard. I chose her poem "Craving" to feature with mine, as both are sort of an *ars poetica* to relationships. And since I mentioned her "passion for poetry" above, I thought it was fitting, we were both writing about desire with a poetic touch.

KELLI RUSSELL AGODON

The Rivers Are Flooding and I Am Thinking about Desire

Today I recited the blackbirds, put their afternoon
alarm on a loop and waved to the hourglass
lilies reminding me that this is as young as I'll ever be.

Yes, your fingers are on me. Yes, you think I'm as dark
as blossoms, but there is no explaining, I am the ink
in your favorite pen and I like having you here, sleeping

on a couch of a paper and books. Sometimes you try
to correct my typos, my catastrophes where the messy
hour is freshwater touching saltwater, and yes, the rain

keeps apologizing to what spills over, but the queen
blossoms are floating and ready. Hold my shady halo
and invite yourself to my side, we can try to bail out

the landscape with coffeespoons, we're poets who
unpunctuate the forest, we have our erasers ready,
though we know we'll never be able to correct the world.

KATERINA CANYON

Craving

I want you to crave me
as you crave caffeine
the first thing in the morning
after a hard night's sleep.

I don't know what it means
to be wanted like that.
I just know what it means
to want, to desire, to be hungry.

I sketch my world in pencil
so that I can erase it
if it doesn't please you,
yet yours is indelible.

I memorize every mood
of your face and trace
them along the nerves
of my spine, to learn

what pleases you.

I have done this for so long
I forget what pleases me.
All that I taste between my
lips is bitterness.

I blame myself more than you.
My world is just filled
with gray smudges now.
I have to find a way

to start over.
Use a new sheet of paper
maybe, and a fine pen,
maybe a Mont Blanc?

I think I might like that.

Featured Poet: Arthur Rimbaud

Harar, Ethiopia, 1883.

The "Missing Elsewhere" as Compass of the Imagination: Arthur Rimbaud's Genius

by Mark Irwin
Paris, 2019

Who was Arthur Rimbaud? Certainly, this is one of the most difficult and complex questions. The precocious poet—companion of Verlaine and Germain Nouveau—who wrote "The Drunken Boat" and *Illuminations*? The soldier deserted in Sumatra? The coffee, spice, and hides trader stationed in Aden and Harar? The arms dealer for King Menelik of Shoa? Certainly, he is the locus of all these people, these places, including the illusive Zanzibar, a quest that he never attains, but dissolves into—through his own complex poetic metaphor: "Je est un autre" (I is someone else).

Born on October 20, 1854, in Charleville, to Marie Catherine Cuif, age 29, and Captain Frederic Rimbaud, age 40 (stationed in Lyon), Jean-Nicolas-Arthur Rimbaud was one of five children, the second son after Frederic, along with three sisters: Victorine-Pauline-Vitalie, who was born in 1857 and died a month later, Vitalie (II), born in 1858 and who died at the age of seventeen, and Isabelle, born in 1860, with whom Arthur would later become very close.

Arthur Rimbaud was six years old when his father, usually absent, finally deserted his wife and family, leaving them in a state of poverty. Arthur's mother, a farmer's daughter, was an arrogant, stubborn, and strong-willed woman who strictly schooled her children. Rimbaud once referred to her in a letter to his schoolfriend, Ernest Delahaye, "as unyielding as seventy-three lead-helmeted administrations."

Arthur, the brightest of the children, began formal schooling at the Pension Rossat when he was eight years old, and in 1865, at the age of eleven, entered the Collège de Charleville where he began to write verse in Latin and French, and was recognized as a brilliant student, winning first prize in Latin—along with awards in other subjects—

in addition to the prize for best overall student. Here in 1870, Rimbaud, now fifteen, meets Georges Izambard, a new professor, under whose tutelage and friendship the young poet flourishes and publishes his first poems.

After the beginning of the Franco-Prussian War, Izambard left the college and Rimbaud became restless and depressed. He left for Paris but was imprisoned there for not paying his train fare. Rimbaud returned to Douai for a few weeks, staying in the Gindre household (the sisters-in-law of Izambard), until Izambard sent him rail fare for the return to Charleville. At this point the frenetic and restless pattern of leaving and returning home—one that will continue all his life—begins. He returns to Charleville where his overbearing and worried mother again sets the stage for the poet's flight. In Charleville, Rimbaud read the Parisian poets, including Paul Verlaine, whom he discussed with his school-friend Ernest Delahaye, before departing to Paris, in order to join an uprising against the peace accord. Once again penniless, Rimbaud wanders the streets, living at times in post Franco-Prussian War garrisons, where some suggest that the poet's first sexual experiences occurred at the age of 16. During this time Rimbaud writes the emotionally exasperated "Coeur Supplicité," while he lives a life of squalor and often rants against the church and women. It is also during this time that he most certainly reads Baudelaire's *Les Fleurs du Mal* and is introduced to Paul Verlaine through Charles Bretagne.

Since much already has been written about the profound and tumultuous relationship between Rimbaud and Verlaine, I'll simply comment that the intellectual freedom that Rimbaud discovers through Verlaine is soon stifled by Verlaine's melodrama and dependence. And Verlaine of course is fed up with Rimbaud's capricious antics. The *on-again off-again* relationship in London ends when Verlaine hints at suicide and their breakup in a farewell letter received by Rimbaud there on July 5, 1873, after Verlaine had left. The letter, dated 3 July, is filled with *faux finales*: "without doubt I had to leave, and this violent life, with its scenes to satisfy your whims, could no longer go on—driving me fucking mad." And later in the same letter, "I loved you immensely ... but ... if in three days I'm not back with my wife and all is perfectly well, I'm going to blow my face off."

Verlaine then changes his mind and is about to return to London but is not sure how he'll be received by Rimbaud and other artists who've witnessed their relationship. On July 7, Rimbaud receives a telegram from Brussels, in which Verlaine hints at joining the army and asks Rimbaud to come to a hotel. Verlaine and his mother are at the Hôtel de la Ville de Coutrai, and when Rimbaud arrives, saying that he will "return to Paris," thus threatening Verlaine's marriage in a more persistent way, Verlaine shoots Rimbaud (July 10) just above the wrist. —Shoots him with the same suicide-intended weapon, which results in Verlaine going to prison and Rimbaud returning to Roche, the upstairs farmhouse room where he will record the trauma in *A Season in Hell*. —The same room that he will insist to inhabit 18 years later after his leg is amputated.

We got along and—inspired—we worked together. But sometimes after loving one another he would say: "How odd it will seem when I'm no longer around—all that you've gone through. No arm beneath your head, no heart to rest upon, no lips over your eyes. For it's meant that I go far away, very far, one day. For I must help others too. It's what I do. Not that it won't be difficult . . . dear heart . . . "[1]

Later, Rimbaud will not encounter such drama with his lesser-known poetic companion, Germain Nouveau, but he will also not be able to rely on Verlaine's wealth and generosity. The Rimbaud-Verlaine drama, which finally involved meetings between Rimbaud's mother and Verlaine's wife (if you can imagine), exacerbates that pattern of return-to and flight-from Charleville and the family farm in Roche where *Une Saison en Enfer* begins whole heartedly in late summer 1873, when Rimbaud returns there and is unable to help with the harvest due to his wounded wrist, but writes furiously instead. The book, which was privately printed and paid for by his mother, was dismissed by many French poets who had an allegiance to Verlaine.

Nothing like *A Season in Hell* had ever appeared in prose, though it roughly follows the prose line of Bertran's *Gaspard de la Nuit* and

Baudelaire's *Les Fleurs du Mal*, while its rants, confessions, and spleen sometimes resemble those of the unnamed narrator in Dostoevsky's *Notes from the Underground*, published in 1864 (also translated as *Letters from the Underworld*). Rimbaud's sometimes visionary, sometimes melodramatic book is uncontainable, too vast for its covers, and its lack of appeal to others turned Rimbaud into an artist who would now geographically seek the visions of which he had written— almost in a kind of strange and dilated *performance art*—as if this had more validity.

Yes, it is after *A Season in Hell* that Rimbaud's identity changes. In late 1873, he befriends the poet Germain Nouveau in Paris, and in March of 1874 the two friends (and possible lovers) will travel to London and live near Waterloo Station, probably at 178 Stamford Street, and it is here, only a year after finishing *Une Saison en Enfer*, that he writes and recopies, perhaps with the help of Nouveau, most of his *Illuminations*. —An amazing emotional and literary recovery! And glimpses of London reveal themselves in poems such as "City":

> Likely, from my window, I see new, ghostly figures rolling through thick and eternal smoke of coal fires, —our shadow of the woods, our summer's night! —hellmongers, hip-Furies, in front of my cottage . . .

Disillusioned with poetry, and becoming more interested in languages and science, he will travel to Germany in 1875; it is here that he sees Verlaine for the last time and hands him a batch of papers containing the manuscript that will become the *Illuminations*. The brilliant "After the Flood" appears first in the original edition and its emphatic, poly-imagistic wave, suggesting as do other poems a new-*Genesis*, eclipses the emotional angst of *A Season in Hell*. The poet, now pure idealist, envisions new worlds, as in "Historic Evening," since he has exiled himself impossibly from real, unlivable worlds:

> When for example on some evening the unknowing tourist finds his of herself apart from our economic horrors, that touch of the master's hands brings to life the harpsichord of the fields; some play cards at the bottom on the lake, a mirror

reflecting queens and favorites. There are saints, harmonic weavings, and chromatic legends in the expiring sun.

In April of 1876 he leaves for Vienna, where he is robbed and forced to return to Charleville, but in May of the same year he enlists in the Dutch Colonial Army, which will take him to Rotterdam, and from there aboard the *Prins van Oranje*, he will sail to Naples, and from there to Sumatra, where he deserts in August, and under the pseudonym Edwin Holmes (according to some), finds passage on the *Wandering Chief*, a Scottish vessel headed for England. One recalls the visionary passages from "Le Bateau Ivre," written by the fifteen-year old poet of piercing emotional perception, a poet who was a surrealist long before others. He literally attains in his voyages to Java—(including the stormy voyage back to England), Egypt, and Abyssinia—what he dreamed in his early poem "Le Bateau Ivre," partially inspired by the work of Jules Verne and written without having seen the sea:

I know the lightning-shattered sky, water
Spouts, reckless waves and currents. I know
Evening, and morning light lifted on wings
Of gulls, and sometimes I've glimpsed what many

Claim to've seen. I've seen the oblong sun, cloud-dusk-
Stained, illumined with long violet shades clotting
Like actors' ancient purple robes, their waves
Shuddering back with those of the sea.

I have dreamed the night, green and snow-
Dazzled, lifting its kiss to eyes of waves,
The circling drift of unknown saps, phosphor's
Waking call, singing its blues and yellows.

After spending the winter of 1877 in Charleville, he tries unsuccessfully to enlist in the American Navy (under the name John Arthur Rimbaud), and then works for the Loisset Circus, which he follows to Stockholm during the summer before returning back to Charleville in August. Within the last three years, the poet has logged in over 30,000 miles through various modes of transportation while visiting a dozen countries! That autumn he departs from Marseilles for Alexandria but must be taken ashore due to a gastrointestinal fever, and when a doctor in Italy treats him, discovers that a rib had worn through the walls of his abdomen from excessive walking!

Much has been made of Rimbaud's walking, which some claim was more than 20 miles a day, and more in Abyssinia. One story related in the Berrichon biography tells of the midwife returning to find the baby—laughing—headed for the door! Rimbaud's friend Delahaye, with whom he walked the environs of Charleville, best describes the poet's unusual gait:

> "His large legs would take calm and formidable strides, his long arms dangling in rhythm with his regular movements, torso and head erect while his eyes stared off into the distance, his entire face bore an expression of resigned defiance, an air of being ready for anything without fear or anger." [2]

It was on similar walks with Delahaye that the two would often find a stopover at a restaurant or bar, one perhaps similar to that described in "Au Cabaret-Vert."

> For over a week I'd torn up my boots
> from the pebbles along the road. Getting into
> Charleroi at the Cabret-Vert, I asked for some
> bread and butter, for some half-chilled ham.

In 1878, he will travel to Italy, crossing the Alps' Saint Gotthard Pass on foot. A keen sense of Rimbaud's resolution and tenacity in hiking into the beyond can be found in the letter he writes to his family from Genoa, Italy, on November 17, 1878, a day after his father, Captain Rimbaud died.

> . . . Here it is! Not a shadow above, below,
> or around us, although we are surrounded by enormous
> objects. No more road, precipices, gorge or sky: nothing

but white to think about, to touch, to see or not see, for it is impossible to raise your eyes from the white annoyance you think is the center of the path. It is impossible to raise your nose against such a biting wind, with your eyelashes and mustache like stala(c)tites, with your ears torn, your neck swollen. Without the shadow that you have become and without the telegraph poles that follow the supposed road, you would be in a big fix like a sparrow in an oven.

Here's something we have to plow through that is more than a yard deep and almost a mile long. We haven't seen our knees in ages. It's irritating. We're panting, for the storm could bury us in half an hour without too much trouble; we encourage each other with shouts (one never makes the ascent except in groups). Finally, there is a roadman. It's 1.50 francs for a bowl of salted water. [3]

In late 1878 the poet leaves for the Alexandria and—due to his language skills—attains a job in Cypress, the Potamos area, where he oversees a quarry, but returns one last time to Charleville after contracting typhoid. After returning to Cyprus in 1880, he will never see his literary friends again and his life ranges between what Steinmetz terms as "rage or mute silence." [4] Now his face becomes somewhat emaciated as he grows a scraggly beard, and the once remarkable blue eyes take on a grey tint. On Mount Troodos, he oversees the construction of the Governor's vacation home, and later while working for a construction company, Ottorino Rosa recounts Rimbaud's story that he killed a worker, accidentally, when throwing a stone during a dispute. Somewhat earlier, while working in a quarry where he must settle quarrels, he requested a dagger. Inarguably there is a pattern of anguish that begins in Rimbaud's childhood, formed somewhere between the overbearing mother and absent father—one evident in earlier poems—that migrates into his relationship with Verlaine, and farther into his working life in Abyssinia, where this anguish transposed into violence seems almost a thing required in order to survive.

Considering Rimbaud's life and poetry, one recalls Emily Dickinson's lines "I dwell in Possibility— / A fairer House than Prose—"

Certainly one sees how in his best poems, like "Le Bateau Ivre," not only does the scene imaginatively unravel, but the metaphor is also continuous—opening up below, like Dickinson's work, into eternity:

> But really, I've wept too much. Dawns
> Rip the heart. Moons devour. In suns I expire.
> Love's butchery has left me drunken and
> Blue. That I might shatter and become the sea!

Rimbaud's poetry moves with ease among the physiological (heart), psychological (Love's butchery), and the eternal (sea). And like Dickinson, Rimbaud displays uncanny gifts of synesthesia along with an ability to make abstract concepts tangible. Compare Dickinson's mortal consequences of light—

> There's a certain Slant of light,
> Winter afternoons—
> That oppresses, like the Heft
> Of Cathedral Tunes—
>
> Heavenly Hurt, it gives us—
> We can find no scar, [5]

—to Rimbaud's hard-won yet playful convictions near the end of "The Drunken Boat."

> Flame-doused, smoking, free, alive with the violet
> Fog, it was I who pierced the red-blushing sky
> Like a wall bearing delicious jam for poets,
> Lichens of sunlight and drooling azure;

What becomes clear is that both poets frequent the beyond to find ontological clarity, and that the "Heavenly Hurt" that Dickinson experiences is amplified in Rimbaud and presented like some communal "jam" for artists. How important it becomes for both these poets, almost contemporaries, to seek possibilities of mortality and religious affliction through language.

One key to Rimbaud's work lies in his complex notion of "eternity," related to an uncanny sense of poetic and personal freedom, a mantra found in his brilliant poem "Eternity," who's first stanza reads:

It's been found again.
What? – Eternity.
It's the sea
gone off with the sun.

But it's the poem's third stanza that is often poorly or mistranslated, which provides an insight into the poet's moral compass and refusal of all convention, whether social, religious, or personal.

From what all
humans think and feel,
you must be free
and fly off as you will.

Only possibility is pregnant with the "now" and this is the poet's key to becoming "absolutely modern." His "drunken boat" courts the beauty of "shipwreck and disaster" where his bark "might shatter and become the sea!" (Ô que ma quille éclate ! Ô que j'aille à la mer!) Or as Emily Dickinson tells us in an early poem from 1859:

Exultation is the going
Of an inland soul to sea,
Past the houses—past the headlands—
Into deep eternity—

Beginning with Rimbaud's physical work as a foreman and a trader in Cypress, Aden, and Harar, the once-poetic desire for "Possibility" is replaced by a constant lust for change. Letters to his family in Charleville are filled with references such as "I won't be staying here long" or "I haven't found what I thought" [6] as he continues to ask for dictionaries, scientific manuals, and even the foreign papers left by his father in Charleville. Before he begins his more lucrative commercial life in Harar with Pierre Bardey, Rimbaud writes to his mother, asking her to send over 25 books on varied scientific, engineering, and craft subjects that included metallurgy, mining, artesian wells, steamships, tanning, and candle-making, and as Graham Robb colorfully observes, "It was the reading list of someone who was planning to start their own country." [7]

The once intense pursuit of poetry, exchanged for one in commerce, seems almost unfathomable to the imagination, but Rimbaud's growing fascination with science in the late poetry perhaps provides a clue, along with the early rejection of *A Season in Hell* and his notorious reputation. It's important to remember Alain Borer's observance, summarizing Mallarmé's, that Rimbaud "was not so much a poet as someone who passed through poetry, as through a thousand other projects always in search of something else." [8] After trading coffee, ivory, gold, cotton, silk, and gum, Rimbaud mounted a caravan through dangerous territory, delivering rifles to King Menelik, a perilous journey and affair in which he was finally cheated. Rimbaud's desire to "trouver quelque chose à faire" (find something to do) no matter what, becomes unsettling, and one cannot help but recall the lines from *A Season in Hell*: "I'm terrified of all trades. Masters and workers. They're all peasants." Envisioning his own fate always seems to make it more tragic. Rimbaud is now measuring his success by wealth. Fluent in several languages and with a strong knowledge of Arabic, Amharic, and Oromo, he becomes in Harar a highly successful businessman who imports and exports a wide variety of products and also acts as a negotiator, guide, and banker.

Jean-Luc Steinmetz notes that Rimbaud's "relationship with money" is a distinguishing characteristic of the years in Africa. Rimbaud's earlier life of poverty is replaced by the idea of fortune. In his letters he says, "I will have gold." "Gold should be seen here as the secular substitute for the sun he once sought as the ideal in a poetic quest." [9] Unlike his world of poetry—fluctuations between inspiration and inebriation—the world of business allows no digressions. Business is predatory by nature; even more so in ruthless North Africa where the margin between predator and prey can vanish in an instant.

As he often becomes frustrated with a business life surrounded by "dogs and thieves," he continues to quest for geographic possibilities instead of those once so easily fulfilled in poetry. Rimbaud's problems are now psychologically real and haunting, and to solve them he must continually conjure a new paradise where trade will be lucrative and unthreatened: "No possibilities remain here"—"If I leave this area, I will probably go down to Zanzibar." Zanzibar becomes his imaginary refuge, one about which he will continue to obsess. Sadly, one cannot help but recall Cavafy's memorable lines from "The City":

> You said, "I will go to another land, I will go to another sea.
> Another city will be found, a better one than this.
> Every effort of mine is a condemnation of fate;
> and my heart is—like a corpse—buried." [10]

The final lines, well-rendered by Rae Dalvin, sum up—with piercing agony—Rimbaud's dilemma:

> There is no ship for you, there is no road.
> As you have destroyed your life here
> in this place, you have ruined it in the entire world. [11]

Those close to Rimbaud are of course his faithful assistant of eight years, the young Djami Wadai, who was with him up until the time of his final departure to France. In the trading factory in Harar, where many gathered, including Djami, stories were often exchanged in three languages. Djami's duties included helping Rimbaud to prepare and accompany him on caravan trips. In his will, executed by Isabelle, Rimbaud left Djami the sizable sum of around 3,000 francs. Without question, Djama and Isabelle seem the most dedicated to Rimbaud.

It is also notable that Rimbaud kept a female servant in Aden, a Christian-Abyssinian woman named Myriam, beginning in April, 1884. According to Francoise Grisard, Alfred Bardey's servant, Rimbaud was intimate with this woman, treated her with great respect, took her out in the evenings, and had plans to marry her. She learned French from him, dressed often in a European style, and smoked cigarettes. According to Francoise Grisard (Bardey's servant), Rimbaud lived in a separate house with her, near the one where he originally stayed with Bardey, his employer. Rimbaud sends the woman away unexpectedly, however, after a little over a year, declaring bitterly in a letter to

Augusto Franzoj dated in September, 1885, "I've had this masquerade before me for long enough." One recalls here his retorts to Bardey and others who had discovered his French fame as a poet—replies that varied from "absurd, ridiculous" to "hogwash!"

These strange events seem to recall the many masks of the former poet, now trader. In Harar, we learn more of his ascetic life from letters in which he claims that he *never* smokes, and drinks nothing but water. The camera that he had shipped to him in 1883, with which he was originally fascinated, was only used for business, making money, though he did initially plan to use it in work for the Geographical Society of France in connection with exploration and map-making. Something that never came to pass. Odd that a former artist of such intensity would not use it to depict warring tribes, plague, the severe landscapes, or profiles of natives (one portrait of a coffee trader exists, along with his own selfie!), but he dismisses this possibility and moves forward just as he has done with previous ventures and business deals.

His famous comment (in the letter to Delahaye) "Je est un autre" (I is someone else) is a complex poetic metaphor, somewhat dislodging Descartes' ego-centric "I think, therefore I am." Rimbaud suggests that the artist transposes the self toward what he or she channels and expresses. One sees this fractured "I" ricocheting, splintering into colors in his famous poem "Vowels," discussed later here. Rimbaud says, "J'assiste à l'éclosion de ma pensée: je la regarde, je l'écoute..." (I assist with the birth of my thought: I look and listen to it). The world traverses Rimbaud's "I." It is also a lens to the reality of Rimbaud's evolution: through suffering and a "derangement of the senses," the "I" becomes a subconscious "I" of the world. Now it appears that his new *life-work* as a voyager/trader in North Africa has taken the place of poetry, or his *art-work*. It is this *l'oeuvre-vie* of Rimbaud that is the most perplexing.

The Bardey brothers described him as often being morose, silent, and withdrawn, while others in the trade business claimed that he told riveting stories, often funny in parts, yet he himself never laughed. As Alain Borer mentions, it's interesting to juxtapose the early Parisian image (of the long-haired, bohemian poet with enticing blue-eyes) to the photo of the haggard, "mummy-like figure" with cropped gray hair and eyes faded gray by the intense sun. In doing so, Borer precisely observes "the rabid need to deny his former body." [12] Yet as late as 1890, four years before his death there are the contradictory letters back to his mother that reveal his protean character: "Could I come home and get married next spring? [...] Do you think that I will be able to find someone who will consent to travel with me? I would like to have an answer to this question as soon as possible." [13]

The tragic end of Rimbaud's life, though narrated many times, is always surprising, for the once-poet, now trader, was always in control. And ironic that he voyages far to the place where all human/hominid life possibly began—in order to die. By the beginning of 1891 Rimbaud suffers extreme pain in his right knee, a pain so bad that he begins to conduct and conclude business from his bed, and by the end of March the pain is so excruciating that he decides to be treated in Aden. Rimbaud designs his own civière, a stretcher in which he is painfully transported 200 miles across the desert to the port of Zeila. The intense suffering from this trip is recorded in his daily log. The diagnosis from Aden reveals cancer in the right knee, and finally on May 9th he sails for France aboard the ship *L'Amazone*. Arriving in Marseille on May 20th, he is taken to L'Hôpital de la Conception where he writes his mother, who remains alone at the farm in Roche and *never* comes to the hospital. Here, on May 27th, his right leg is amputated. He is later fitted with an awkward prosthetic, which he hates. The tragic summer of the same year involves Rimbaud, accompanied by his sister Isabelle, traveling by train to Roche on July 23. The pain is so intense that he is often lying down, passing in and out of consciousness. Patti Smith precisely captures the agony in an early writing:

his lightweight wooden limb lies against the wall
like a soldier leisurely awaiting orders. the master,
now amputee, just lies and lies. gulping poppy tea
through a straw—an opium syphon. once, full of
wonder, he rose in hot pursuit of some apparition—
some visage. perhaps harar a heavy sea or dear
djami abandoned in the scorched arena-aden. rimbaud rose and fell with a thud. his long body naked

on the carpet. condemned to lie there at the mercy of
two women stinking of piety. rimbaud. he who so
worshipped control now whines and shits like a colic baby. [14]

Partially paralyzed and losing control of his arms, he travels back
to Marseille, again with Isabelle, in delirious hope of sailing back to
Aden, but he becomes totally paralyzed and is hospitalized again in
Marseille. He finally dies on the 10th of November, after having ac-
cepted confession (deliriously no doubt), in the presence of his sister.

The intense suffering toward the end of Rimbaud's life seems to
bear witness to the rebellion of having been locked inside one body.
The poet was always breaking literary/human bonds and moving to-
ward the "essence of life," which was either the sea or the sun. Jacques
Rivière most aptly called him "a monster of purity" and Alain Borer
notes that "most of his poems celebrate exploits." [15] Not surprising,
Verlaine characterizes Rimbaud as a self-disinherited European, a
cultivated savage and explorer who never looks back on what he loved
in flesh or verse. Verlaine, who in a way gives birth to Rimbaud, can
never really declare him dead: "Yes, dead! But you live in me with a
thousand fires . . ." [16]

Finally, and most important, Rimbaud, more than any poet of his
era, redefines place. Alain Borer speaks persuasively of the *L'ailleurs ab-
sent* (missing elsewhere) in Rimbaud's life and writing. Borer notes that
the word "ici" (here) is constantly used in his letters. It seems that the
poet is hopelessly trying to locate himself; and finally, in a letter from
Aden, he writes "La vraie vie est absente." [17] (The true life is absent.)

Again, this is the poet who would often walk up to 25 miles a
day, both in Europe and Ethiopia. In France, the poet used to read
and sometimes write while walking, a notion that makes "place" a
kind of *pregnant now* where not only the body is moving, but words,
phrases, finding their more vital syntax. "Lis ceci en marchant" [18] (Read
this while walking), Rimbaud advised his friend Delahaye. Through
voyages to England, Germany, Austria, Italy, Java, Egypt, Sudan, and
Ethiopia—yet often finding no real pleasure in any of them—Rimbaud
creates a radical vision of the "l'ailleurs absent," the missing elsewhere
that he could only sustain in his imagination. See his many letters of

fleeing to Zanzibar, "where things will be better." He detests in many ways his hometown of Charleville ("my town is the center of idiocy among all the other towns of the province") to which he often returns, yet he also complains of Cyprus, Aden, and Harar. Rimbaud is only happy within a kind of *nature in motion*, which he embodies. One experiences a keen sense of this at the *Maison d'ailleurs* (part of the Rimbaud Museum in Charleville), the house where Rimbaud lived for a time as boy and budding poet. Polyvocal sounds (trains, doors, rivers, along with scraps of speech) infuse multiple locations throughout the house's rooms.

In Rimbaud's brilliant *Illuminations*, multiple locations are sensually located in the present then denied. Here's an example from "Après le deluge" (After the Flood):

Blood flowed, at Bluebeard's house—in the slaughterhouses, —in the circuses where God's seal of light blushed windows. Blood and milk flowed.

Beavers labored. Coffee cups steamed in the bars.

In the mansion-like house with humid windows, children in mourning gazed at marvelous pictures.

A door slammed, and on the village square, the child waved his arms, understood by weathervanes and wind cocks everywhere in the dazzling rain.

It's as if Rimbaud, by locating and denying place, finds a universal present. He is in fact like the child "on the village square" who waves his arms and is understood "by weathervanes and wind cocks" in all possible directions, *everywhere*. This is the true genius of Rimbaud and it is no different in his poem "Voyelles" where he invents colors for each vowel. Why? —Certainly, out of a frustration with the limits of language. Color *does not* evolve in a manner similar to words through the grammatical rules of language. Color is much more ancient and primal. Its language comes from the human body, earth, sky. Color is at once physical and metaphysical: red from blood or fire; blue from sea or sky. In "Voyelles" the poet not only invents the colors but tells of their origins:

> The black A, white E, Red I, green U, and blue O: Vowels,
> someday I'll tell of your dormant birth: The black
> A's hairy corset of shining flies which buzz
> and buzz around such brutal stench
>
> in shadow-gulfs; The E's white of vapors and tents,
> tall, lancing glaciers, white kings and supple flowers;
> The I's purples spit blood, laughter of alluring
> lips angry or sorrowfully drunk.

—Just as in "After the Flood," we sense that the notion of place is *displaced*. The vowels become colors, the colors in turn something else: "The black / A's hairy corset of shining flies which buzz / and buzz around such brutal stench / in shadow-gulf..." As with much true genius, the poet's impatience burns from silence. Rimbaud is working sublimely in a field of color that Rothko will expand on 100 years later.

All of this brilliant invention recalls the poet's love not just for science but for some *new science*, something that he speaks of in "Lightning" from *A Season in Hell*: "—What can I do? I know what work's ahead; and science is too slow." Remember that in the same poem's prologue, the poet tells us that after sitting "Beauty" on his knees, "I found it bitter." This poet who finally reckons that *beauty* would destroy his life? —One only salvageable now through travel, business, science? Yes, and in this work's last section, "Farewell," he tells us: "One must be absolutely modern." It is Rimbaud's obsession with *the new* in all things that makes him great, that drives not only the poet, but the *traveler*, the *trader*, and the *explorer* who extend the limits of the word —and the *world*—with *his* spirit and with the physicality of his body, what he called *free freedom*.

Mark Irwin
Paris, 2019

NOTES

1   All translations, unless marked otherwise, are by Mark Irwin and are based on the following French Edition: Arthur Rimbaud, *Oeuvres Complètes*, Bibilothèque de la Pléiade eds. A Guyaux and A. Cervoni (Paris: Gallimard, 2009).

2   Jean-Luc Steinmetz, *Arthur Rimbaud: Presence of an Enigma*, trans. Jon Graham (NY: Welcome Rain Publishers, 2001), 223.

3   Steinmetz, 246.

4   Steinmetz, 249.

5   Dickinson, Emily. *Complete Poems. of Emily Dickinson*, ed. Thomas Johnson (Boston: Little, Brown, 1960), 36.

6   Steinmetz, 277.

7   Robb, Graham. *Rimbaud: A Biography*. (New York: W.W. Norton, 2000), 316.

8   Alain Borer, *L'heure de la fuite*, trans. Mark Irwin (Paris: Gallimard, 1991), 95.

9   Steinmetz, 265.

10   Constantine Cavafy, *The Complete Poems of Cavafy*, trans. Rae Dalvin (NY: Harcounrt, Brace, 1976), 27.

11   Cavafy, 27.

12   Alain Borer, *Rimbaud in Abyssinia*, trans. Rosmarie Waldrop (NY: William Morrow, 1991), 168.

13   Steinmetz, 351.

14   Smith, Patti. *Early Work: 1970–1979* (NY: W.W. Norton, 1994), 102.

15   Borer, *Rimbaud in Abyssinia*, 271.

16   Paul Verlaine, *Dédicaces* (Paris: Vanier, 1894) 139. Note: Inspired by a drawing by Isabelle Rimbaud, that shows her brother in Eastern garments.

17   Borer, *L'heure de la fuite*, 83. Letter from Aden, 1885.

18   Borer, *L'heure de la fuite*, 76.

Harar, Ethiopia, 1883.

ARTHUR RIMBAUD translated by MARK IRWIN

The Drunken Boat

(1870–71)

As I was going down wild Rivers
I lost guide of my deck hands.
Yelping Indians had targeted and nailed
Their naked bodies to colored stakes.

I cared little for any of the crew, whether those
Of Flemish wheat or English cottons.
And when the ruckus and confusion ended,
The rivers gave green wish to my descent.

I—another winter—ran, dumb and aloof
As any spacey kid into the furious
Lashings of tides. Loosened peninsulas
Never survived a more-wild assault.

The storm blessed my sea-skills.
Lighter than a cork I danced on waves,
Those eternal wheels of the dead—for ten nights—
Without missing the lighthouse's stupid eye.

Sweeter than the crisp flesh of apples
Is to children, green water soaked
My bark, rinsing me of blue wine and vomit
While loosing the rudder and grappling hook.

And from then I bathed in the Sea's
Poem, bleeding with stars, and milky,
Devouring the azure-greens where sometimes
Pale flotsam resembles one who slowly drowns;

Where delirium, slow and rhythmical,
Stronger than wine, longer than a guitar's held
Chord, suddenly bleeds through blue, streaking
Daylight, distilling love's sour red.

I know the lightning-shattered sky, water
Spouts, reckless waves and currents. I know
Evening, and morning light lifted on wings
Of gulls, and sometimes I've glimpsed what many

Claim to've seen. I've seen the oblong sun, cloud-dusk-
Stained, illumined with long violet shades clotting
Like actors' ancient purple robes, their waves
Shuddering back with those of the sea.

I have dreamed the night, green and snow-
Dazzled, lifting its kiss to eyes of waves,
The circling drift of unknown saps, phosphor's
Waking call, singing its blues and yellows.

I've followed the sea-cycle's pregnant swells
Hysterical as cows howling at reefs
Without dreaming that any Mary's luminous feet
Could tame the ocean's wheezing snout.

I've pitched against magnificent Floridas
Where flowers seem panther eyes with human
Skin, where rainbows arc their bridle reins
Beneath the sea's horizon toward greenish herds,

I've seen great swamps ferment, fish-traps
Where a Leviathan rots among reeds!
Torrents of water splice a calm so-close;
The far-away cataract toward whirlpools!

Glaciers, silvered-suns, pearled waves, dusk-
Charred skies! Brown gulfs issuing toward
Impossible strands where giant serpents devoured
By bedbugs drop from gnarled, stinking trees!

I would've liked to show children those sun-
Struck fish of the blue wave, fish of gold, singing
Fish. Flowers of sea-foam cradled me
And incomprehensible winds winged me at times.

Sometimes a martyr, vagrant, fed up with poles
And zones, the sea whose sob created my gentle roll
Brought me dusk-flowers with yellow suckers,
And I remained like a woman on her knees . . .

An island's guess-work, tossing its sides
Among quarrels and the scat of noisy,
Yellow-eyed birds. Yet I sailed on while drowned
Men sank back to sleep through my fragile hold.

Tossed by storms into the birdless air,
I was lost in the foliage of coves, a boat
Whose drunk carcass would not have been rescued
By Monitors or the Merchant's League.

Flame-doused, smoking, free, alive with the violet
Fog, it was I who pierced the red-blushing sky
Like a wall bearing delicious jam for poets,
Lichens of sunlight and drooling azure;

Who ran, spotted by small incandescent moons,
A plank, wild, escorted by black sea horses
When Julys rained down their hammers
And the skies, ultramarine, burned with funnels;

Who puppeted by fear heard rutting
Whales and spitting whirlpools from fifty leagues,
Who spins eternally heaven's blue stance, and who
Misses Europe with its ancient parapets!

I've seen archipelagoes peppered like stars! and islands
Whose delicious skies open to the sea nomad: In these
Depthless nights do you sleep beautifully
Exiled—a Gold million birds—a Future's pulse?

But really, I've wept too much. Dawns
Rip the heart. Moons devour. In suns I expire.
Love's butchery has left me drunken and
Blue. That I might shatter and become the sea!

If I dream a water, it's Europe's, the black
Cold puddle where a child sadly squats
And releases into the twilight
A boat fragile as an insect's wings.

Lazily draped in the sea's waves, I can
No longer follow in the cotton boats' wake,
Approach the swagger of flags and flame,
Swim under the awful eyes of prison ships.

Translated from the French by Mark Irwin. An earlier version originally appeared in *The New England Review*, 2001.

ARTHUR RIMBAUD translated by MARK IRWIN

Seven-Year-Old Poets

(1871)

And closing the school workbook, the mother
leaves satisfied and very proud but unaware
of the loathing that seethes within her son's blue
eyes—and under red lumps from slaps on the brow.
All day long he sweated obediently—so very
smart he was—yet bad habits and certain traits
seemed to reveal so many hidden lies at work!
In shadowed hallways with damp paper,
he stuck out his tongue in passing, two fists
in pants pockets, and saw floaters in his closed eyes.
When a door opened toward evening, by lamp
you'd see him high up, groaning on the stairway
where daylight still flooded through the roof.
In summer, pissed-off, dazed, and stubborn,
he'd shut himself up in the cool outhouse,
where breathing deeply he could think in peace.

When washed from day's scents in winter
and the small garden behind the house filled
with moonlight, he would lie at the foot of a wall,
buried in clay, rubbing his dizzy eyes hard for the visions
as he listened to the scabbed espaliers creaking.
How fucked! His only friends were those bare-headed
and puny kids with eyes sunk into their cheeks,
the ones who hid thin fingers—yellow and black
with mud—under old clothes soiled with shit.
Kids who talked such sweet-crap. Dopes!
And if mother caught him doing cruel things,
she was shocked, but the boy's tenderness
would win her over till it was OK. She
had that cold-blue look about her—that lies!

133

At seven he was writing novels about life
in the great desert where far-freedoms lie,
forests, suns, riverbanks, plains! —He was helped
by newspaper-pictures, and blushing over them
saw giggling Spanish and Italian girls.
When the daughter of workers next door
came by—eight years old, brown-eyed, in a calico
dress—the little brat jumped him from behind,
shaking out her long hair in a corner, and then
under her, he bit her ass since she never wore
panties. —Bruised by fists and heels, he
carried her skin's wild taste back to his room.

He feared those gloomy December Sundays
when—hair slicked back on a mahogany stool—
he read from a Bible with cabbage-green margins.
Each night dreams stifled his small upstairs room.
He didn't love God but those tuff, dusk-guys
in leather jackets he saw returning to the suburbs
where the town criers with a triple drum beat
got the crowd laughing as they made fun of new rules.
—He dreamed of prairies, their luminescent swells,
where musty scents gave way to gilded sexual pangs,
ones that kept stirring to rise in the too-still air!

And especially keen on all things dark,
he sat up in his bare room, high and blue-lit behind
closed shutters where sour—sweaty, he read
over and over his novel full of heavy ochre skies,
sopping forests with fleshy blossoms opening
in astral woods. —Dizzy pages of collapse, rout, and pity!
—Above noisy streets of the town he lay alone
on sheets of unbleached linen breaking violently into sail!

ARTHUR RIMBAUD translated by MARK IRWIN

Ancient

from *Illuminations* (1872 / 1873)

Slick son of Pan! Around your forehead, flower and berry crowned,
the precious spheres of your eyes move, and stained with wine
dregs, your cheeks grow hollow. Your fangs gleam. Your chest is
like a big guitar and a ringing flows through your blond arms. Your
heart beats in this stomach where the double sex sleeps. Wander
through the night, moving gently this thigh, this second thigh
and this left leg.

ARTHUR RIMBAUD translated by MARK IRWIN

Mystic

from *Illuminations* (1872 / 1873)

On a mountain's slope, angels twirl their woolen robes
across pastures of steel and emerald.

Meadows of flame leap toward one round hill. On the left
that ridge-crest has been trampled by every murder and battle,
and all the horrid sounds still file around. Behind that ridge on the right
lies the line of ascent, progress.

And while this picture's top frieze is formed from the turning,
leaping hum of conch shells and those of human nights,

The sweetness of stars blossom with sky and the rest
descends—opposite that mountain slope—like a basket against
our face, and creates an abyss, flowering and blue down there.

from *L'Œuvre-vie et la métanoia d'Arthur Rimbaud*

Arthur Rimbaud's Life-work and Spiritual Quest

by Alain Borer, 2020
Translated from the French by Mark Irwin

TRANSLATOR'S NOTE:

In the following essay, when Alain Borer discusses the four theme phrases (*me in a **hurry** / to **find** / the right **place** / and the **formula**/ **way***), he is noting a pattern of key words that continue throughout Rimbaud's correspondence, and that also refer to the last line from Rimbaud's poem "Vagabonds": "moi pressé de trouver le lieu et la formule." It is a last line that more correctly suggests in its translation: "me always impatient to find the right place and way by which to live." Borer is also noting a pattern of key words that continue throughout Rimbaud's correspondence, words that outline an obsession for an *ailleurs*, or a *somewhere else* that Rimbaud is always in a hurry to find, and in that new place—a new way by which he might live. The following selection from Alain Borer's essay ("The rebel figure") references a regular pattern in correspondence (primarily here from Rimbaud to his family) that illustrates this haste for an *impossible elsewhere*. The theme words within brackets have been capitalized and inserted by Mr. Borer in order to illustrate his thesis. The first Rimbaud letter excerpted, May 4, 1881, provides an excellent example ("*I'm going to buy a horse and then go away*"), which commits to this thinking syntax (*Hurry-Find-Place-Formula*) or the syntactical as an act. I have also reprinted Rimbaud's defining letter of November 2, 1870, to Georges Izambard, which emphasizes the poet's obsession with *la liberté libre (free freedom),* a defining character of both the poetry and obsessive searching in his life.

There are multiple allusions to Zanzibar, a compass point that Rimbaud is never able to attain, except in the imagination, and thus I chose it for the title of our book: *Zanzibar: Selected Poems & Letters of Arthur Rimbaud.* In his essays, Borer employs a style of paragraphs often divided by semi-colons, a style that often heightens the impatience and desperation of Rimbaud's search.

Mark Irwin

moi pressé de trouver le lieu
(me hurrying to find the place)

Arthur Rimbaud never stopped walking. Don't imagine it any differently through the streets than on the "running white road," "the great road in every weather," the paths and mountain ascents, in deserts and in snow. The total for his entire life: about sixty thousand miles. Rimbaud is the one Verlaine called "*the man with shoe soles of wind*" and the one who dies early with his leg cut off at the hip.

His first poem in Latin ("Election of the Poet" 1868) foreshadows this: "my limbs broken by my long wanderings…" Neither textualism (for which walking is at best a theme) nor biographers (for whom writing is a Seated Act) have integrated this first evidence: the constant *Rimbaud-march*. The Rimbaud-tradition represents on the contrary a period of "wanderings" in his life from 1876–77, which would succeed the literary enterprise, journeys taken after his poetry!

However, when Rimbaud wrote in one of his very first poems in French (1870): "I will go far, very far, like a gypsy…", he's really playing truant and "writes" this poem while walking ("*I was plucking some rhymes / on my walk*"), and a letter to his teacher Izambard attests the same, "endless walks, bohemian journeys" (August 25, 1870);

during long fugues or endless ballads with his school friend, Delahaye, the boy (as brilliant at school as he was at truancy) would initially walk on foot to his hometown, Charleville, whose city plan was an ideal of the 17th Century, and then he would wander into its region, the sumptuous Ardennes that sported names in the form of walking goals: *Élan, La Bascule, La Cachette*…;

then he made it to Paris on foot (two hundred and forty kilometers, finding seven different residences in seven months) and when he stayed in London with his companion "of hell," *every day*, according to Verlaine, *he took long hikes in the suburbs and countryside.*" Travel does not take the place of poetry: both began together, inseparably—with always this pressing need to "*read and walk a lot*" that Rimbaud communicates to Delahaye. In Marseille, in July 1891, reflecting on his past as he suffered, crippled in bed, Rimbaud wrote to his sister: "*In Abyssinia, I always walked a lot . . . excursions of 10 to 25 miles a day . . .*"

How many times will he have taken the *number eleven train*? This is slang, representing the two fingers, the index and the middle finger, which humorously suggest *walking*— and which meant during that time about two hundred and forty kilometers . . . On the coast of Zeilah, the hocks of the donkeys were cut when they arrived from the highlands of Harar, after two hundred and fifty kilometers of winding road.

A letter from Berrichon (the future posthumous brother-in-law) asks Isabelle: "At his trading post in Harar, until 1891, did he remain sedentary?" And the sister's exact answer: "He told me he had crossed the desert eleven times." The route cut by donkeys, eleven times: and the caravan here was the same sign as that of the *eleven train*— walking, always.

Didn't he say it himself? "I'm a pedestrian, nothing more." In the poems too, "At the Green Inn" or in *The Illuminations* you see him passing: "*I'm the pedestrian of the highway by the sapling woods; the rumor of boat-locks covers my steps. For a longtime I've seen the sunset's melancholy gold-wash.*" An endless march to the inaccessible place.

The *here* never satisfies him—Charleville, "*outstandingly stupid among all provincial cities*" or Aden that he would like to see "*reduced to dust, rubble*"! The *elsewhere* is the superlative of *here*. Elsewhere takes all kinds of names, a dozen or sometimes twenty names of different places in each letter, for twenty years. We must connect "*a road of danger*" in a draft of *A Season in Hell* with the "road of dangers"in several letters from Abyssinia: it's the same road that crosses the poems and letters, "the white road" where Rimbaud's steps resound;

Aden . . . , Brussels . . . , Cairo . . . , Jeddah . . . , Entotto . . . , Fumay . . . , Gilbraltar . . . , Harar . . . , Insbruck . . . , Java . . . , Kombarovan . . . , London . . . , Marseille . . . , Naples . . . , Obock . . . ,

Paris..., Queenstown..., Roche..., Stuttgart..., Utrecht...,
Vienna..., Warambot..., Xylophagou..., Yabata..., Zeilah...

or Zanzibar, an alphabetical equivalent for the voyage that Rimbaud conceived several times (in 1887), the next stage of trade shipping boats, from Aden to Zanzibar, an image of the inaccessible elsewhere, the port always beyond...:

thus a map of *elsewhere*, unsatisfied and infinite, Scotland and Ireland both considered with Verlaine for the summer of 1873, the United States, Japan, China..., and Zanzibar becomes the name of "these magnificent lands where the existence of a thousand men would not be enough to visit" (January 15, 1885), the ideal Rimbaldien place, distanced by compulsive movement, which we might call the *prolocation*.

According to the constantly expanding map of *Rimbaldia* (a map in anamorphosis / one changing as he moves), the walker infinitely approaches these "splendid cities," referenced at the end of *A Season in Hell* as the "*splendid cities*"—these which do not come after his major poetic work, but—on the contrary—arise from the first poems ("Sun and Flesh," 1870).

The dimension of *place* in "this former schoolboy's truancy" (Verlaine, 1888) is the wandering as much as the quest, as in the word *querrance* (in the sense of heaven, closed, definitive, inaccessible as suggested in Spanish querrancia). This is how infinite Rimbaldia becomes: or in terms of singular logic, querrance is the object of prolocation...; thus, prolocation is to space what impatience is in time, the same figure of the Impossible.

This place sought everywhere and carried forward could only be that of deliverance and *the new body*. This ambition is measured by physical and mental suffering when in 1891, before his death in Marseille, he had so much trouble getting his *one remaining foot* into *one* shoe. "Who can grab hold of a mirage? asks Apollinaire. And he's always mistaken, the one who believes he's filling his arms with divine love!"

The rebel figure: Arthur Rimbaud

by Alain Borer, 2019
Translated from the French by Mark Irwin

It has not been measured just how much Rimbaud's life becomes a *rebellion*: it supports absolutely no constraint, no order, no relationship of superiority, no obligation to anyone, anybody (*quiconque*); life for Rimbaud is just absolutely *impossible* in any regulated or civilized country, even in companionship with relatively close poets.

Just as we can recognize these *theme–words* in his life, in acts or in the *synacts*, without doubt they probably structured the essence of Rimbaud's lost conversations . . . : they therefore become the major signifier—and a great one, *extended* but not heard for nearly twenty years, disproportionate to any other consideration, literary or biographical—to understand Arthur Rimbaud.

If the letters of Africa and Arabia could seem "sacrilegious" to Camus (in *The Rebel*, 1951) because he believed that they merely stated the commonplaces and trivialities of the real, the boredom or the despair rather than the "poetry," it's merely for wanting to hear *that*, which is said and repeated constantly, uniquely, when listening to the theme-word, that is to say the signifier where the fundamental and constant model weaves and reweaves itself:

this major signifier, immense and permanent (much longer than the poetic enterprise), presents a scientific character, insofar as the main criterion of the science rests on the predictability: it is foreseeable indeed that in the next letter of Rimbaud, and in every next sentence of this letter, the four theme-words will be organized; it's even by this trait that we recognize an Arthur Rimbaud letter.

This pattern, with an authority superior to any other appreciable element, answers the question *who is* Rimbaud: he is the one who was always hurrying to find the place and the formula. Hurried (*Pressé*)? This is the dimension of time, the question *when*. To find (*Trouver*)?

That's the question of the thing, the question *what*. The place (*Lieu*)? It's the dimension of space, the question where. The formula (*La formule*/model/way)? It's the question of the means, *how*.

Here are several excerpts from letters containing the four theme-words that illustrate this Life-work pattern:

1881, HARAR, MAY 4

Personally, I plan [FORMULA]to leave [FORMULA] this city [HURRIED] soon [PLACE] to begin trading [FORMULA] in some unknown parts [FIND]. **I'm going to buy a horse [FORMULA] and then go somewhere [PLACE].** (*Translator's bold*) Can one find work [FORMULA] in Panama [PLACE]? Be well. I'm off. . . [HURRIED]

1882, ADEN, JANUARY 18

I left Harar [PLACE] and returned to Aden [PLACE], where I wait [HURRIED] to break my contract with the trading company [FORMULA]. I'll easily find [FIND] something else [FORMULA].

1883, ADEN, FEBRUARY 8

I spent a lot of money [FORMULA], but I'll get it back, and then some. Send me only the books [FORMULA] that I've asked for; don't forget them [HURRIED]. I will certainly leave Aden [PLACE], and I will write to you before. All best to you [HURRIED]

1884, HARAR, JANUARY 14

I barely have time [HURRIED] to greet you since the company is making me liquidate this agency [FORMULA] in Harar [PLACE]. It's likely that I'll leave here, [PLACE] for Aden [PLACE], in a few months [HURRIED].

1885, TADJOURA, DECEMBER 3RD

I'm here [PLACE] to organize my caravan [FORMULA] for Choa [PLACE]. It's not going very fast [HURRIED], as usual here. The merchant-stuff [HURRIED abbreviation] we import [FORMULA] is obsolete, almost worthless rifles (with 40-year-old cocking chambers).

1886, TADJOURA, JANUARY 2ND

I'm always busy [HURRIED] in Tadjoura [PLACE] and will certainly be for several more months [HURRIED]; my business is going smoothly [FORMULA]. It takes superhuman patience [HURRIED] in these countries [PLACE]. I'm still waiting [HURRIED] for that book [FORMULA]. My departure here [PLACE] is still somewhat delayed [HURRIED]; so much that I doubt that I'll get to France [PLACE] this autumn. Wishing you well . . .

1887, CAIRO, AUGUST 24

My dea(r) [HURRIED: abbreviation] I need to ask you a favor [FORMULA]. Soon I must take the Suez ship to Zanzibar [PLACE] because I'm told many opportunities [PLACE] await there, while here [PLACE], though I can always find [FIND] something [FORMULA], life's too sedentary [PLACE], but in Zanzibar [PLACE] we could travel toward the interior [PLACE] and live for nothing [FORMULA]. So, I'll go to Zanzibar [PLACE] and there [PLACE] I'll have many opportunities [FORMULA], not to mention the [FORMULA] recommendations that I can get in Zanzibar [PLACE]. I will leave my money here [PLACE] in the bank, as there are traders in Zanzibar [PLACE] that do business with Credit d * [HURRIED: abbreviation], and I will always get interest on it [FORMULA].

1887, ADEN, NOVEMBER 5

I'm always preparing for something [HURRIED]. I wait [HURRIED] for answers from different places, to know where [PLACE] I'll take myself. There may be something to do [FORMULA] in Massawa [PLACE]. Yet I'll not be long [HURRIED] making a decision [FORMULA] or finding [PLACE] the job I hope for [FORMULA]; and maybe I won't leave, neither for Zanzibar [PLACE] nor elsewhere[PLACE]. Tell me what's the most important [FORMULA] newspaper in the Ardennes [PLACE]? Best to you [HURRIED].

1890, HARAR, FEBRUARY 25

I don't want to lose my ass here [PLACE]. I do business with a Mr.Tian [FORMULA], a great merchant from the city of Aden [PLACE].

1890, HARAR, APRIL 21ST

I have neither the time [HURRIED] to get married [FOR-MULA], nor am I interested in getting married. For me it's absolutely impossible to leave your business [FORMU-LA] in these devilish countries.

1890, HARAR, AUGUST 10

May I come [PLACE] to get married [FORMULA] at your place [PLACE] next spring [HURRIED]? But I can't agree to stay with you [PLACE], nor to leave my business dealings [FORMULA] here [PLACE]. Do you think that I could find [FIND] someone who would agree to follow me on my journeys [PLACE].

1891, MARSEILLE, MAY 30,

to His Excellency the Ras Mékonène

I write to you from Marseille [PLACE]. I'm in the hospital. My leg was cut off six days ago. I'm good now and in about twenty days [HURRIED] I will be healed. In a few months, I plan [FORMULA] on returning to Harar [PLACE], to do business there [FORMULA] just as before.

To Georges Izambard: Charleville, November 2, 1870

Sir,

—This note to you alone. —
I returned to Charleville a day after leaving you. My mother welcomed me, and here I am— . . . just idle. My mother wouldn't put me in boarding school until January of 71.
Well! I kept my promise.
I'm dying here, decomposing in the dullness, in all the bad and gray weather. What can I say, I stubbornly and fiercely adore *free freedom*, and . . . a lot of other stuff that's "a bit pathetic" right? —I needed to leave today; because I could: I was dressed up in new clothes, I would have sold my watch, and all for freedom! —Consequently I stayed! I stayed! —and yet I'll want to leave again many times. —Come on, let's go, hat, coat, both fists in my pockets, and we're off! —But I'll stay, I will stay. I didn't promise that. But I will do it to earn your affection: you told me so. I will deserve it.
The gratitude that I have for you, I could not express it today more than the other. I'll prove it to you. It would be doing something for you, that I would die for it, —I promise that. —I still have a lot to say . . .

This "heartlessness" of A. Rimbaud.

War: —No siege of Mézières. But when? We don't talk about it. — I gave your commission to Mr. Deverrière, and if more needs to be done, I'll do it. Here and there, outspoken tirades. —Abominable shows of idiocy, such is the spirit of the people. We hear it from the best, come on. It's all falling apart.

Kwame Dawes

Romeo Oriogun

The locution, "in the cold of the world, we sharpened our bodies / into dance" is exactly the kind of strange alchemy with struggle and pain that Romeo Oriogun is perfecting in his poetry. He is, to my mind, revitalizing the elegy. "Elegies are one of the few places where we can do the work of care, not just to ourselves but to our dead ... Grief is always naked, but it has the capacity to clothe those who are gone ..." He opens here a window to the truly distinctive poetic vision that he is developing in himself, one that grows out of experience, that grows out of a deep sense of the sophistication of the ancient traditions of Nigeria, and the urgency of a poetry of the moment. I am saying that Oriogun is part of a remarkable cadre of African poets who are transforming the global poetic landscape.

KWAME DAWES

For Rainford Lee "Scratch" Perry

On mornings of reggae, spongy as the body in repose,
the dreams of desire and the taste of curried goat two days old,
the rice grainy, softened by the coconut oil of sweetness,
I fail at language to describe this bass-line, for the spaces
it fills and the way the body softens to its graces.

And here I sit surrounded by the fat rhythm and melody
while a grainy-voiced upsetter runs his eloquent
trap with the fully formed discourses of mystery and livity—
dipping and turning back—over the sallow earth of the boom
sound. Think what history is lost in the silence of sounds
made only to vanish into the ether—as if the meaning of time
is the meaning of truest silence—what we record is the stain
of memory. Try, and all we have is language to construct
the vanishing of noise.

                 The old reggae man has built a shelter
deep in the mountains of Switzerland, and there he steps
into the blue mornings, glowing with the inner light of snow,
and there he howls symphonies, the recollection of his being,
into the sky, and he does so in faith, though knowing
that every howl is an elegy for the dearly and un-dearly departed;
it is an elegy for the dubs he has constructed and discarded
in pyres, the tapes melting away, the skeletons of the reels
blackened and melted in a midden, the place where he has kept
the surplus toasters that kept arriving by morning mail,
long after he had completed the grand Rasta wall of toaster,
("not a boaster"). And on a night of sleeplessness, he opens
the sound system and lets the tape roll. In a trance
the riddim is made—he lays down his autobiography
against Babylon, his autobiography against silence—
first the stone, the boulder with eyes glaring out,

then the horses of white, and sorrel and red, stomping
in under the cypress trees; then the priest squatting in the temple's
backyard, waiting for the visitors to arrive with the news,
though they never arrive. Where is the head corner stone?
The Spiderman a-come, he says, *The superman a-come*,
sun is shining, the weather has changed, I rearrange, I rearrange.

ROMEO ORIOGUN

Ballet in the Cold

after Rita Dove

Behind the rainforest we watched the stream,
its slow run through the deep cut of earth.
The night was alive, the stars burned
like little fires finding life through the dark path
filled with trees. The wild flowers,
the call of baboons, all forerunners
of the ruin that awaited us.

That night, death was far from us,
the day was a stranger. The gramophone
inherited from my grandpa was silent,
a dead musician teasing us from his grave.

We were naked like the day of our conception.
In the cold of the world, we sharpened our bodies
into dance, we committed ourselves into the void
of mystery. And now that the arrow of time
has been let loose into us, we must remember
that night, nature rising within us, baboons
returning to the glorious shade of trees, walking
through bush streets where the first man found fire,
iron, the brutal end of wood, devoting himself to war,
the beginning of borders, the beginning of exile.

Linda Bierds
Elizabeth Bradfield

For as long as I've known her, Elizabeth Bradfield has seamlessly fused her primary callings, that of a poet and that of a naturalist. Her experiences at sea in Alaska, the Eastern Canadian Arctic, Antarctica, or Cape Cod's outer reaches have found vivid, haunting expression in her books, particularly *Approaching Ice, Once Removed* and *Toward Antarctica*, and in the pages of many magazines, including *The Atlantic Monthly, Poetry*, and *The New Yorker*.

"Today, Alongside" is filled with the tension I so admire in Elizabeth's poems, a complex layering marked by precise description and what refuses to be contained by description. I found myself stair-stepping down to the poem's declared subject, the humpback whale—first introduced in italics via metaphor, "big wing of New England"—passing on the way what might be seen as the poem's inner subject: the fusion of the tangible and intangible. What flits in so many trochees across the poem's first lines? Storm petrels, walking like the apostle Peter over the water. And music. And ghosts, present and past.

When incantation yielded to anecdote, I was with the speaker and the dead whale—and held, however briefly, by the act of enjambment that gives "pandemic" so much weight. As sharks fed on the carcass, I circled the tangible, flocked to its fodder. I had entered the cycle of nourishment and decay, but as a voyeur, a participant only through the imagination's intangible terrain. And what other tangible intangibles were—are—hovering so close to me? What, by the poem's end, am I breathing in? What dissembled ongoing am I now a part of?

LINDA BIERDS

Captain Scott's White Ponies: A Cento

—South Polar Expedition, 1910

They are so silent, they are of another world,
thing of shimmer, thing of shine,
a fragment repeating repeating a kind of shudder.

An impossible condition with ponies,
the first sheer ice, black, then white,
the fearful marches through eternal snow.

Down in the yellowing underworld,
a crowd of ghosts will come and stand
all the way into the water,

no galactic rose at the center
like a small, beating flame that suddenly
astonishes.

Snow, it is morning.
What are the animals, the land,
a spawning ground for polar ice

but now steaming and glistening under the flow of light?

The eye can hardly pick them out.

Always the light falls,
while they drift farther away in the invisible morning,
dropped in some wilderness of the broken world.

Lines by D. H. Lawrence, Elizabeth Bradfield, Ellen Bryant Voigt, R. F. Scott, Gail
Mazur, Richard Wightman, Norman Dubie, William Ogilvie, James Wright, Karl
Kirchwey, John Engels, James Richardson, Dan Beachy-Quick, Michael McGriff,
Elizabeth Bradfield, Ted Hughes, Philip Larkin, Kenneth Patchen, W. S. Merwin,
Edwin Muir.

ELIZABETH BRADFIELD

Today, Alongside

—*Megaptera novaeangliae*

Flitter over water over
fat-slick, gobbets plucked,
water pattered, dark souls
of storm petrel (of sailors)
restless and hungry and
able to walk on water.
                    Up-slick,
the body, now carcass, now source,
belly up. Whale I watched
a year ago as calf, as hope
in that first, uncertain pandemic
summer, nursing with his
mother, nursing from
his half-fluked mother
(Venom) who had survived
something else borne
before I knew her
that took one part
of how she travels.
And now this:

              Undersurface
ripple then fin then shark
          a great white rides up
          the throat-slope—blubber
wobbled, grabbed, torn. Water
now blooded. Hunger met. Another
              shadow-glow circles, feeds. Another.
      We gawk.

Nodal point in all the gulf's
waters at this moment, you gather

us. We flock. You are forage, fodder,
are other than we imagined. The sea calms
downtide from your flank, oiled
smooth by what you slough.
And, stink thick and coating,
we take you in. We watch, we
breathe, we are now part
of your new, dissembled
ongoing.

Lynn Emanuel
Deborah Bogen

In the post apocalyptic garden that opens Deborah Bogen's "Reconstructing the Crime," the snakes have multiplied until they *glide through the rubble like new forms of water*. This powerful poem, from the manuscript of her fourth book, *Speak Now This Charm*, manifests Bogen's characteristically nuanced and complex manner of presiding over tragedy. "Reconstructing the Crime" describes the drone bombing of civilians, and, rather than preside over such material from the comfort of indignation, anger, or even compassion, Bogen walks herself totally into the scene. And she takes her reader with her. At the end of the poem the bombed civilians, the narrator, and the reader are inconsolably and inextricably bound together and are one in the rubble.

LYNN EMANUEL

After Three Weeks at the Museum

I saw the figures of the crucifixion in sexual terms.
A virgin is weeping, He is asleep, eyes closed,
dead to the world.

The same old story—mind and body—
a marriage on the rocks. He is already dreaming of the great
angels of the resurrection. She is unable to reconcile herself.

Who killed him? Somehow, she seems implicated,
simply because he's dead and she is living.
Her sorrow illuminates these works.

But her lamentation is businesslike. As though
she knew all along she would outlive him.

DEBORAH BOGEN

Reconstructing the Crime

If you remember anything—it's the drone-whine, that omen of
conflagration and crumbling. Of snakes gliding through rubble like
new forms of water. Dust curtained the air, but there was no sound.
Just a void where there should have been roofs falling, bones breaking,
bloodied bodies crying out. What a hell-shaped silence. The village
dogs pantomimed barking.

What you remember is your own fucked-up focus. The way you sat.
Drone-struck. Stupid. The way your mind wouldn't work. Your mind
became a river that slid snake-like out of that scene. You didn't notice
the scratched-cornea vision or the bits of broken rock and glass that
filled your mouth. None of that mattered. A great fatigue had arrived.
And it sat you down.

Maggie Smith

L. A. Johnson

L. A. Johnson wowed me with her poems at the 2021 Indiana University Writers' Conference, and she is still wowing me. In "While I Wait for a Late Train at Union Station," I admire how she tests how elastic a stanza, each a single sentence, can be: what it can hold, and how we unpack it. I admire the masterful enjambments, which help us parse the syntax, providing both suspense and sly wit: "approximately / forever" is perhaps my favorite break. I admire the music in the word choices—the way "little spills" chimes against "hillside," and the way the assonance, consonance, and alliteration ("chaparral tangled," "the perfume of pears") feel organic to the poem, not merely ornamental or overdone. I admire the imagery, and in particular the attention to texture—those Manzanitas like "gifts / half-opened and then abandoned"; "the rough skin of a roasted chicken." I also admire the tension between the title and the poem. The simultaneity, the "meanwhileness," is so compelling. Even the word *late* in the title, such a small adjective, points to the expectation of order that the world described refuses. I've become a fan of Johnson's work, and I'm always excited to see what she does next.

MAGGIE SMITH

Because

When I think of God watching me,
if there is one, which I waver on, I hear

a deep sigh. Of disappointment?
Impatience? Surely God knew

I'd lose a pound for every year I lived
as a wife, once I wasn't one—good years,

some of them, but the last few were last
for a reason. Surely God knows

that, too. And the questions I carry
without answers to make them whole.

If there is a God, I'd want to ask,
Why did you let me starve like that?

And God would know I mean it
metaphorically, mostly. Instead I ask

myself, in whom I believe, more
or less, and I try to make a whole

by answering. *Why, why, why*
is one half. *Because, because, because,*

the other. When I think of God,
if there is one, the sigh I hear

is my own. Why? Because.

L. A. JOHNSON

While I Wait for a Late Train at Union Station

        Little spills of poppies cover
the dry hillside without rainwater,
orange like the fire-danger warnings
aimed to high alert approximately
forever out here where nobody clears
away dry brush, chaparral tangled
and the red skin of the Manzanitas
curls off like the wrapping of gifts
half-opened and then abandoned,
while what's left underneath waits
to burn.
           A coyote,
eyes the color of dead leaves
falling against a window pane, paces
his territory of burnable things,
looking for a comfortable patch
of clover to lie down on, where wind
carries the perfume of pears ripening
in wicker baskets and rough skin
of a roasted chicken, until the risk
of sleep feels less dangerous,
like a lover's name in the mouth.

                My heart beats
dumb with discovery: wonder
won't exist until it's made.

Martha Rhodes
Rushi Vyas

I am always interested in how poems in manuscripts can inform other poems through revealed and withheld narrative—how one poem might lead to what is revealed in another poem, and another, and another—and how the poet manages to build upon both story and emotional narrative through use of lyric, diction, syntax, image, figure among other important craft tools. Vyas, in his forthcoming collection, *When I Reach for Your Pulse*, weaves many tethers into a stunning, cohesive collection and this poem is in conversation with so many other poems in the book—thread, noose, father, blood—are core words in this short poem—words that hit hard because as the book is read as a whole, we learn that the son found the father dead by a hanging suicide. This poem speaks to birth identity and inheritance (what the son is left with in terms of memory) and ultimately gives us insight into how the speaker begins to find his way through the laws of different cultures and thus discovers and and reckons with his own destiny—or at least begins to.

MARTHA RHODES

Seen through glass,

the eyelash magnified. Also, sperm. Swimming, like all of us,
I thought, I thought, nowhere—hamsters on a wheel.
Husband's seed speeding away from me. I saw
the barren-ness of the future when at that time
even the word "my" coupled with daughter, son, house,
plate, headache—"my" plunged scalpel-sharp into the heart
by well-intentioned friends—as in, *My Ben turns 10 today*—
sending me to the inner skull's roof, a cliff to leap from,
yes, until, I suppose, after decades, I just became
deafened to, and by, the word. And when I look at the world
through the glass of the microscope on the loved one's curious desk,
to discover what the dampness of a paper towel reveals,
the mind is flat as a jellyfish fried on Miami Beach sand.
I was once there with parents, rich enough for the Fountainbleau,
its Shirley Temples and umbrella'd virgin drinks all for *me*,
and that wondrously glorious pool, empty at noon save for Father
who we all watched through the surprising glass wall at our first buffet
there, along with other guests, pointing, laughing, then ready
to harpoon him as he, oblivious, pulled off his trunks and performed
that underwater dance. A few teens jumped in, saw, and raced away
from the excited milky water (I'm imagining that detail).

What brings me to the microscope today—certainly not sperm.
Peanut butter smeared, just peanut butter. Drop of diseased blood,
unreadable to me. A dead cat's whisker retrieved from safekeeping.
Dull, perhaps, I never see anything more than what's evident.

RUSHI VYAS

Midwest Physics: Third Law

at the Bob Evans on Harvest Lane
Bapu ordered his western omelet
no ham and I told him I was dropping
out of medical school
foreclosing on my debt

my country teaches   for any refusal
retaliation   on the ride home from school
after 9/11   a white man flipped us off
our evasion   *we are Hindu*

how brahmin   the slide step
how american   the elision
perhaps these laws stretch
beyond borders   undetained

perhaps we're pulled like waves
by an unseen mass in day   and light
is never swallowed by dark
but only grappling with its refusal

Bapu's fork scraped the plate
a Jay alighted on a power line
beside a pair of red sneakers swaying
under the noose someone tied of their laces

under the moon in May's blue sky
I swirled pancake in the maple's blood
Bapu tried and failed   to say
all my hard work   for you to become a bum

now that he is gone   what's my equal
and opposing force?   for each omission
between us dear father dear country   what's the word?
for every noose   someone must cut the thread

Maurice Manning

Nathaniel Perry

Nathaniel Perry's poem, "A Property in the Horizon" is from a series of poems, each with the same title, and each composed in quatrains of diminishing meter—5-4-3-2. Based on what I've read from the series, the poems record and respond to the poet's daily life in rural Virginia, yet the poems give that life the oomph of extra life, conveying the sense that what's going on is always more than the record can relate. I certainly enjoy encountering this effect, which is not additive, but geometric, and wonderfully ironic, given Neil's approach to a diminishing form—less in this case is certainly more. There is a compelling clash between the outward push of content and the shrinking form. Form and metrical lines are key elements of composition that signal and create such an expansive poetic vision, and Neil's work is all about a rich poetic vision that goes beyond mere sight. This is the work of a consummate craftsman, solid and distinct, and attached to the vitality of being human in this world. When a poet uses a nonce form, over the course of many poems the best result is a cumulative expression, and in this particular series from Neil, the form enables wonder to reach beyond its limits.

I would pair Neil's poem with a so-called double sonnet I've spent time with in the last couple of years. Although my poem doesn't follow the sonnet's conventional rhyme scheme and the lines are 4 beats instead of the usual 5, I think we're in similar territory poetically, in terms of attention to rhythm and rhyme and how those efforts influence the total effects of the poem. This is what I love about sharing an intuitive vibe with Neil. He's on his place in Virginia and I'm on mine in Kentucky, yet we labor on common ground.

MAURICE MANNING

The Knot

I have a complicated knot
I won't untie that lives on a loop
of string with another loop twisted
or wandered through it, as if the loops
belong to each other but it's not
easy to see how they are joined.
My father tied the knot long back,
some year when I didn't know him
when I didn't think he knew himself
or me, or would imagine now
the moment of my study, not
untying anything about
the knot he tied that now outlives him,
and sits there living on the string.

The double loop, the knot, the string
he tied with purpose and made this thing,
designed, I think, for doubling.
What else to do but study it,
to see the silent hitch and sing.
Old Man, I see your hand in mine
and in it something rare and fine.
I like a hitch in the line, like you—
my little art is doubling, too.
And you were just a lonely man
with a string and a pair of sleepy hands
who made a knot with two loops through it
to remind me without saying so,
you longed for love and tied me to it.

NATHANIEL PERRY

A Property in the Horizon

Somewhere in the arms of this morning's fog
my neighbor's cows are alarmed, the boom
and bell-blast of their lowing
like a gong in a room

too small for a gong. Though who makes rooms for gongs?
—whoever makes fog-hollows and knells
for cows, I suppose, and put
in their lungs those bells.

But come to think of it, and of the dawn
they and I are interrupting,
they're probably not alarmed,
but are announcing

instead the hay my neighbor's bringing in
on the front-tines of his tractor. It just
sounds like fear when I factor
out their trust.

Michael Waters

Yesenia Montilla

The Latin phrase, "per aspera ad astra," generally translated as "through hardships to the stars," may have originated with Virgil and has seeped deeply into contemporary pop culture through literature, film, and music. In her poem, though, Yesenia Montilla claims it for herself, making of it less a metaphorical motto of aspiration than a literal prescription toward immortality. The poem is understated and modest and "too human" in its "obsession" and muted humor. It's also political in its eco-stance and awareness of our "transgressions." Most of all, though, it's touching in its sadness and yearning and self-interrogation: is it still possible, despite the "nothingness" that surrounds us, to move beyond ourselves into myth?

MICHAEL WATERS

To Marvin

> Marvin Bell 1937–2020
> for Dorothy

The digital display on the bank's new marquee
7:52   8°   7:52   8°   illuminated snowfall
As I tilted into wind icing the river.
Michael! whooshed past my turned-up collar.
Iowa City, Valentine's Day, 1974.
You stood in a doorway & waved
A folder waterproofing a sheet of paper,
A poem to Dorothy,
To be printed & matted & framed
Once the art supplies store opened.
Did I want to read it? Of course.
  You are not beautiful, exactly.
  You are beautiful, inexactly.
I recognized the Shakespearean gesture
From Sonnet 130
["My mistress' eyes are nothing like the sun"],
The one that chastises poets for "false compare."
Still. A risky gambit.
                    I wavered in my response.
The fleeting dots of time & temp
Reddened snow within their airy compass.
A few flakes blew onto the transparency.
We huddled together over the flame of poetry.
O, she'll love it, I told you, not lying, exactly.

YESENIA MONTILLA

Per Aspera Ad Astra

I have a serious problem, I am too human
I am constantly centering myself & believe
I will always exist, if not here, then maybe
on a rover on the moon or a slick colony
        on mars

To imagine life beyond this planet
has become an obsession of mine. Imagining
myself living in the blue of Neptune
is as fathomable as envisioning myself forever
in the arms of my beloved—

& this happens often enough, the dreaming,
which brings me to Orion, who was a killer
of nature, maybe the most human of us all
& he so vexed Artemis that she captured
him in space, to keep a better eye on his
transgressions

Lately, I have been revisiting the stars
Late night when I believe the city sleeping
I step outside & look up into nothingness
A dark city sky—if I cross the street into
the park & wrap my arms around a tree

I can almost hear her whispering something
about how small I am, how tired she feels

The earth seems unhappy or sick or maybe
I am sick & undeserving to sit at its bed side
while it wastes away into nothingness & me
I just keep wondering what gods will be left
after all of this is gone   What gods
        to turn me into a constellation?

Nicole Callihan

Zoë Ryder White

Zoë and I have been writing poems together since the turn of the century. If we are not writing poems together or alongside each other, we are texting each other. Maybe she'll be sitting in her car outside the CVS waiting for the rain to slow so she can run inside to buy plastic eggs to put in a basket, or I'll send a bitmoji of myself in a Jello-mold, but every few days, we come to our perennial question. *What* even *is a poem?!?* One of us will ask. *I dunno*, the other will say. *Hahaha, hopefully we'll remember soon!*

And yes. We will. We do. Anytime I read one of Zoë's poems, I'm like, THAT's a poem. Here, in "Like Louise," Zoë first imagines herself in the rumpled button-down of Louise Bourgeois; Zoë becomes the artist, and then, in the very next line, she *becomes* the art, wrapping the "you" in her many, many arms. And then—relentlessly devoted to the interior—she keeps going, keeps becoming—*the map, the green patch, the meat inside the shell*—and she does so, and so beautifully, in order to muscle closer to "it;" her it being, I think, poetry itself, art itself, our very reasons for making locked inside nineteen clear-eyed, dreamy lines.

NICOLE CALLIHAN

Formal Ambiguity

Before bodies was the spine
of the dime store paperback;
and before Lot's wife turned back,
she had to leave; and before leaving,
there was arriving; before arriving,
the readying, the pins in the hair,
those stockings with the polka dots—
this was when women painted
their lips; before gaudiness; when
love seemed mostly available
to anyone who sought it;
sawdust & rain; *being* not as conceptual,
not as theoretical, but *being* as *being*;
devoid of context. If what is learned
must be unlearned. If emptied,
refilled, but if filled, emptied again.
Something with the timepiece.
To be self-conscious; or to be
conscious of having a self.
Self as postage stamp; as weeping
in bodice; as traded for candy,
other sundries. My mother says,
she is feeling rough & disillusioned;
asks if there is any pain when urinating.
What illusion turns blurry? Dissolution.
Meanwhile. I mix water with powder.
Voila, pancakes. Voila. Breakfast.
Voila. Sated. What I haven't stated
I likely won't. The word sadness
shares its Latin root, *satis*, with
satisfaction. Of fullness. Of having
had one's fill. Which is different
from depression. In such, old French,

the angular distance of a star
below the horizon. In the same way
I might press this pen so hard
to the page, I'll leave an impression.
These things are both countable
and uncountable. Paper, time,
memory. Light, room, hair. Forsythia,
maybe. Mother. Where did you go?

ZOË RYDER WHITE

Like Louise

I want to wear the rumpled button-down like Louise,
to wrap you in my many arms, mid-air,
to be that heavy and that suspended.
Resistance and yield,
yield and resistance.
To wear away what isn't you
to find you, talk to you, tend to you.
I want to dress in black and white like Louise,
to commit to formal ambiguity
as a map to follow
when stepping off the road.
The green patch is the place for couplings,
Untitled.
To have reached up to the shoulder joint
is to have become the meat inside the shell.
To wear the iron crown.
To wrinkle.
To muscle closer to "it," W
to "you."

Nin Andrews
Cassandra Atherton

When asked to select a poet for this anthology, I immediately thought of Cassandra Atherton, an Australian prose poet and scholar whom I've admired ever since I read *Prose Poetry: An Introduction*, published by Princeton University Press in 2020, which Atherton wrote in collaboration with Paul Hetherington. After perusing the book, I looked up Atherton's poetry and thought, *Why didn't I know about her before?* Both an academic and a master (or should I say, mistress) of the prose poem, she is one of those rare writers able to achieve a perfect balance between prose and poetry. Eloquent, witty, clever, and just plain gorgeous, her work is difficult to resist. Many of her poems, like this lovely "Pre-Raphaelite Triptych," pay homage to other artists, effortlessly weaving their vision into her own tapestry of magic and meaning. Dreamy, lush, and sublime, the poem possesses a dizzying combination of eroticism and clarity. Each paragraph hangs like a painting on a gallery wall. If it were possible to crystalize an orgasm and present it on the page, as I have tried too many times to do, Cassandra Atherton's poem serves as a demonstration of exactly how it might be done. A pleasure to read, Atherton's poetry is, to my mind, one of a kind, and deserving of a wide audience in this country and beyond.

NIN ANDREWS

My Father's Prayer

My father hid lovers in his coat pockets,
his office, his dreams. He thought
we didn't notice their scent of aftershave
and cigarettes on his linen suits,
their phone numbers on his dresser
along with the loose change.

He thought we didn't see the way
his eyes followed those men
like a silent flame, tracing the curve
of shoulders, lips, hands.

His favorite, a naval officer, lived for years
in the walnut bureau in his dressing
room, the top left-hand drawer
in a watch box beneath socks and cufflinks.

Sometimes, when my dad wasn't home,
I visited the officer, too. Dressed in uniform,
tall white cap in hand, his smile was faint,
his hair thin, his skin pock-marked
like a chewed pencil. *How ugly*, I thought,
but his words I loved.

They were pale blue on even paler blue
paper that my father had folded
and refolded into an origami cube.
"Last night I dreamt you licked
the wound on my chest
as if it were an envelope,
then pressed it shut."

•

"I've been cured," my dad told my mother
the day he finished conversion therapy.
"Now I can love only you."

My mother looked at him, askance.
"Cured?" she asked.
Isn't that what you do to a ham?"
My father didn't laugh.

•

That night before bed,
when he thought I wasn't looking,
I watched him open the sock drawer,
lift the officer out of his box, and finger
his small black and white image
as if it were holy,
as if it could save him.

I think I knew his prayer.
I could feel it singing in the air.
Let me burn. Let me burn again and again.

CASSANDRA ATHERTON

Pre-Raphaelite Triptych

I. LA BELLE ISEULT

> after William Morris's painting (1858)

In dark rooms, with slow rhythms, he unmakes her. He rests her sideways across the bed. Arched backs, like conjoined parentheses, skin on skin—a blissful roiling and churning. Afterwards, she holds him in a complicated desire to slow the separation of flesh and breath. In a few hours he will travel back across the border, leaving behind their tangled sheets as an unfinished portrait of what they made.

II. LADY LILITH

> after Dante Gabriel Rossetti's painting (1867)

He rings to tell her she left an apple core in the small, green rubbish bin in his bathroom. Red Delicious, with the seeds exposed around its narrow middle, his wife found it three days after she'd gone, decomposing in furry strips and mottled dots on the white flesh. But she doesn't remember apples or offscourings, just kisses on her bare shoulder as she pulled long, orange hairs from her brush each morning, winding them into bright loops. Now she thinks of the hair nesting at the bottom of the bin liner, stuck to a rotting apple.

III. SLEEPING BEAUTY

after Edward Burne-Jones painting (1871)

The third night, they drink too much tequila and he sleeps
on the edge of her hair until noon; his body curled around
her like a single, right parenthesis. She feels his breath
on the rounded curve of her shoulder, respiration like
a steady metronome. This is her happiest hour: three
quarters of a King Size bed behind them, her toes a series
of ellipses under the sheet.

Rae Armantrout

Brandom Som

This poem is both timely and out of time. It communes with the spirit of experimental Tejana composer Pauline Oliveros, who once taught at UC San Diego where Brandom teaches now, and who died in 2016. San Diego sits about 20 minutes north of the Mexican border by car. (Brandom is half Chinese-American, half Mexican-American by birth.) Here he counterposes the gentle, open listening of the musician against the American administration's attempt to silence the other, the immigrant by stringing razor wire. You can't get very near the border now without seeing it. It's interesting that "concertina" got its odd name for the way it folds like an accordion—the instrument Oliveros played. When Som quotes Oliveros saying, "I have experienced listening with my palms," I think of the palms of immigrants grasping the concertina." I also want to say that this poem is as musical as it is about music. Sometimes it sounds like syllabic poetry or blank verse. I found myself counting syllables to check. It's not, or not simply. Still, the last line of the first stanza and the first line of the second stanza are such a beautiful pair, describing Oliveros' experiment with bouncing sounds off the moon: "where it bounced back to her / dropped in pitch by Doppler." Each line there is six syllables and there is also an odd slant rhyme. I'm even more taken with the double p's in "dropped" and "Doppler." This is a poem about attunement—and the lack thereof.

RAE ARMANTROUT

Waves

To know a thing
is to know what it's made of—

> a nest
> made of ants
> hanging by
> one another's legs.

To know a thing
is to know how to make it;

we hope to learn
how to make the world.

•

To make something
you must know where
it began—

> with the shifting
> hierarchies
> of (stuffed) animals,

> > with the sea,
> > a set of
> > jumbled sentences

> > each ending
> > in Ssshh

BRANDOM SOM

from **Tripas**

With ham operator, Oliveros
sent a *hello* to the moon's tympanum
where it bounced back to her—

dropped in pitch by Doppler
effect—& she then accompanied
the echo on accordion. In today's

news, U.S. troops install the miles
of border razor wire, so-called
concertina for the coil that extends

& flattens like the hinged folds
on a squeezebox's bellows. 'Listen to
everything all the time & remind

yourself when you are not listening,'
instructed the Tejana composer
of sonospherics & chi kung student

of quantum physics. 'In practicing,'
she once said, 'I have experienced
listening with the palms of my hand.'

Rafael Campo

Stacy Nigliazzo

Stacy Nigliazzo's poems painstakingly (re-)assemble the piercing, shining shards of the experience of human suffering to imagine the possibility of healing. No detail, no disquiet, no teardrop is too small to escape her attention and care: she is at once nurse and poet, her unflinching hands probing our wounds, her utterly exact words just as skillfully tending to our souls. In "Above His Bed" what she observes in the hospital space brilliantly transcends the literal meaning of the clinical, as "Nothing by mouth" is abruptly understood as the loss of the patient's voice, while "FALL RISK," suspended as it is on its own dizzyingly enjambed line, warns death is always near. As Nigliazzo invites us into such shared intimacies, poem after poem drawing us closer to her work as healer during the COVID-19 pandemic, we too mourn the loss of our voices, and recognize we too are falling—and yet are saved by poetry, which demands as ever "please make eye contact with me." That human connection—eye to eye, hand to wound, ear to chest—is how essential poetry like Stacy Nigliazzo's ultimately and indispensably sustains us.

RAFAEL CAMPO

Scenes from the Field

The land mine detonated, killing two
young women as they planted corn. The field
had seemed so peaceful in the morning sun.

Come fall, we helped to clear spent corn. Too soon
stars spilled like seed across the night's dark field—
so near, our breath unscrolling in the chill.

The plane wreck smoldered over miles of fields.
A farmer found a wig suspended with
the tassels, some surreal portent of corn.

What looked like rolling fields along the highway
was actually an enormous landfill.
No wonder corn they sowed there never grew.

They found a girl's dead body decomposed
behind the strip mall, in what used to be
a cornfield. People whispered she'd been raped.

A single cornstalk stood in center field.
By opening day, it was tall enough
that no one had the heart to cut it down.

My uncle raised beets, strawberries, and corn.
We found an arrowhead once, when the fields
were fallow. Nothing else was left of them.

Some guessed a spaceship; others said it was
a prank. Huge circles carved in fields of corn.
What's strange is you can't see them from down here.

STACY NIGLIAZZO

Above His Bed

Nothing by mouth

FALL RISK

Nods head—responds verbally to daughter Helen (via Zoom)

please make eye contact with me

Ramón García

Ata Moharreri

"We still have prayers to receive in this world," strikingly concludes Ata Moharreri's "Mailbox Blues." I admire the poet's ability to depict a heightened perception with a concentration and economy that is matched by his skilled prosody. Moharreri's sensibility is close to devotional, or reverential, for lack of more categorically precise terms that do not include the definitively religious. His poems seek, they are searching. In his poetry sensuality is fragile yet masculine. Nature is so much a part of human interconnection that it proves to be in danger, or dangerous. There is consistently some sort of unease at the heart of his poems, and yet that is what makes the poems tick, the source of their intrigue and understated complexity.

"Mailbox Blues" borders on the surreal and suggests the mystical. It operates at the margins of the human, the mundane and the cosmic. Depicting the phenomenological world of a North American mailbox, it's a persona poem of sorts, a dramatic monologue that encompasses a correspondence with the landscape, the mailbox's natural surroundings. Who knew that a mailbox could be that enigmatic, that alive? That a household object so ubiquitous and commonplace could contain multitudes of the quasi-symbolic and still have a sense of humor? Is the mailbox a messenger, a conduit for troubled communication, an intermediary between nature and human distance? It's perhaps all of the above (and more) and what poetry gives access to: transcendence and illumination.

RAMÓN GARCÍA

The Sirens

Feminine island voices
Where ocean depths taught them
The dark reaches of silence
And the surf's turbulent conservatory
The superhuman pitch of what has never seen sky
Or breathed air

Legend has it
They have wings
An irresistible speech granted by flight
By the wind and the sea's violent distances

You who must live a flightless gender
Destined to hear your sister-Self multiplied
To be tied to their isolated choir

You were chosen for the dangers of song
To be glorious music's singular brother

ATA MOHARRERI

Mailbox Blues

For Tennessee Saeed Moharreri

I know not every letter sent arrives.
Termites tunnel through soil.
A magnolia tree is to my right.

Night washes over my missing numbers.
I look into a leafless sky
At the bottom of a puddle inside a rut.

"Not all lucky stars get counted,"
The magnolia, stiff and twisted, reminds itself.
In the middle of faded verbena I stand,

My post covered with rime.
A shaving of light brushes against my door.
Mites chew secrets that haven't left the tree.

Three stars disappear, and a barn owl hops
Along a downward reaching branch.
The owl slips on dark without making a sound.

I stand near the chewed up tree
And chatter from the stars keeps the owl awake.
We still have prayers to receive in this world.

Shamar Hill

Carolyn Joyner

"Imagining Warrior" creates an intimacy with the reader with its first two words: Imagine him. That longing speaks to a desire which, I believe, is purposely rendered with a sensuality, but by the end of the poem is dramatically changed; so, on a second read the lines and the poem take on a new meaning. A dangerous meaning. This evocative poem is a magical journey for the reader, crafted line by line in a way that is enthralling and haunting.

SHAMAR HILL

Bathymetry

I.

This story, with the sharpened blade
of memory, is easy to forget,
easier to remember.

She coated a basket with pitch and tar,
placed her son inside with a blanket,
and watched him drift—
a lure below the early fog
among the reeds by the riverbank.

She became weightless when she let him go.

II.

My father became a legend
on stoops and corners.
His cackle and fedoras,
the tilt of his wrist glinted
his gold watch and forties.

He died without dying
thousands of times.
He transformed into
an abandoned building,
prowled my restless nights,
a gray ghost.

I begged him to leave me alone,
almost as much as I pleaded
for him to return.

III.

She looks out at the river, in the distance,
the blunt arrival of this story,
the remembering and forgetting of this story.
She can see it with her eyes,
the land promised to those before her,
that she will not cross.

I look out at the ocean,
the waves gray ghosts,
fixated on my father,
convinced I am a strange accident.

The ocean's ancient eyes, in quivers,
stare back at me, pulling at me
like my first cries hours after
my mother's water breaks.

CAROLYN JOYNER

Imagining Warrior

Imagine him big-framed, packed tight,
standing a head above his henchmen.

Imagine him wearing an extra-large boar's tusk
helmet, untouched by fury's gusts, his warm

bath water self suited under armor, palming
the might of its hand in yours, rugged smile

flashing the small gap in his front teeth.
Imagine his oak tree legs unyielding to force,

clearing thick walls, high fences, on a fine steed,
saddle made especially for him. Imagine him

stumbling upon a narrow tunnel he's compelled
to enter, believing its end holds light, finding

only deeper darkness, surprise attack, fierce battle—
being pummeled pitilessly day after day,

all of his body parts laid open. Imagine him using
bone as spear, gristle as shield while sitting

tall in his saddle, not tumbling from his horse,
never giving up. Imagine his mother witnessing.

Sophie Cabot Black

Tacey Atsitty

Tacey Atsitty's poems are a wonder in their use of music and language, myth and imagery. While Atsitty posits the reader direct into the particulars of the Navaho creation myth, she also casts us into the complicated human lives of communities ravaged by other humans. The figuring of central themes such as lakes and ravines, sky and earth, male and female, monster and mother, are paired both as inseparable and dialectical as the heart (desire) and the body (survival) can be. Atsitty takes from her culture's myths while holding us to the trauma of its more modern history, brings them forward into forms that stride both the ancient and the current worlds—asks us to reach past the seen, while also keeping us in her light, slowing down our tongues. This villanelle, though formally tight, also has a braid that illuminates as it moves. Read this work out loud; it is a joy and honor to be in her room of words. Tacey Atsitty is a master weaver and dancer, and first and foremost a poet.

SOPHIE CABOT BLACK

The Ford

We lost when it began to grow
Into after and became the only

Place we knew. How far we have
Come to rely on chance: the river

Might have shown clear unspooling
In a wholly other spot,

But when my animal came to drink,
Your animal drank along the facing shore

And when they looked up to see
They saw. From the seep of mud, from

Newly fallen trees the trail begins
And in the season when the water slows

Each animal comes close enough
To hear, to smell the other breath, keep

Eye to eye in the narrow footing, now
Overrun, ground-down, to be easily found.

TACEY ATSITTY

When the River Separated Us, We

It was us who created monsters, Eve,
Five-fingers Ones—Diné like you and me.
Tell me, what was it again that we grieve?

Álk'idą́ą́, First Man and First Woman heaved
it out: hot words leaving his body, He—
It was us who created monsters: Eve

at the riverside, throwing clay pots. We've
come a long way since the cornfields, since She—
Tell me, what was it again that we grieve?

Whole nation of genders lost to conceive
from waves, from warm flesh, fresh after a kill:
It was us who created monsters, Eve.

Us who tossed aside cacti and stones. We've
left ourselves: our fingers, our babies: we.
Tell me, what was it again that we grieve?

They survived ravines and ravenous thieves,
but found suck then came back to eat us: We—
it was us who created monsters. Eve,
tell me again, what is it that we grieve?

Steven Cramer

Aaron Wallace

We often don't pay enough attention to a poem's title. Ignoring that doorway into the terrible beauty of Aaron Wallace's "Battle Hymn of the Republic," we'll miss a central disproportion. Cunningly referenced nowhere else in the poem, the title's allusion to Julia Ward Howe's celebrated hymn to patriotism jump-cuts to the first line's intimate exclamation: we feel a vertiginous shift in scale, as if abruptly descending from an aerial establishing shot to a close-up. The poem is replete with such enlivening disparities—rotting roof, rusty pipes, otherworldly acoustics?—but I'll notice here two other, indelible, elements: its character development and orchestration of time.

In sixteen lines, we grow to love this singer whose name means "little dark one." The platoon's mascot, court vocalist, and surrogate parent at bed-time, Kieran also has an exclusive rapport with the speaker. He not only perceives his native talent, but he also intuits that this nascent poet has already posed to himself the Rilkean question—"ask in the stillest hour of the night: must I write?"—and answered "yes." A mentor both empathetic and telepathic. Only after establishing that bond does Wallace introduce another vital quality of Kieran's generosity—the power to make art from art. In a wildly eccentric take on the Keatsian equation, Kieran morphs the speaker's poetic subject—"my ex-girlfriend's sister in a blue bikini"—into a song whose title claims a distinct truth about American eroticism. Bikini is truth; truth, bikini.

For good reason, then, we love Kieran, and our love accounts for much of our heartbreak when he kills himself off-stage. But it's the poem's handling of time and timing that elevates a dreadful death to Aristotelian catharsis. Wallace tells the story of Kieran in the simple past tense, but not all past tenses are equal. In the first fourteen lines, Kieran's singing sweetens the barely breathable swamp air of one remembered summer. In the penultimate line, his suicide occurs in a past-tense flash-forward to the end of that season. Thereafter, the last line's return to prelapsarian innocence releases an almost unbearably poignant tension between festivity and elegy, glaring as the double-faced mask of classical Greek theater. In a stunning instance of dramatic irony, the platoon sings the fruition of Kieran's and the speaker's special bond, necessarily ignorant of what readers now know. The gun just fired can't be unshot, however, so readers must hear the platoon's celebratory hymn as a tragically proleptic dirge.

STEVEN CRAMER

The Look

I'll never tell Ethan I listen to him sing
in the shower. It might make him stop.
I like whoever's singing to keep singing.
I pause at the door until the water shuts.

To some, singing's a sin, a capital crime.
Some, to brighten their afterlives, pack
mirror shards into a pipe, thus boosting
their radius of kills, in song, at prayer.

Have you ever tried talking to a guitarist
as they play? Not on stage, of course,
but in a room where their strumming
consorts with the gossip. There's a look

I'll call *The Look*. My brother (1945–1990),
had it; my nephew—who, for a living,
bivouacs north of the Muir Woods,
making fire with a spindle, hearth-board,

bow, and bearing block—has it too:
a stare aimed through you, blank as sheets
of still-reamed paper, so anything you say
leaves no mark; a mindful mindlessness

where the work of play gets done. Ethan
grudgingly began on a Yamaha acoustic—
cheapest guitar you can buy that's not a toy—
thirty daily minutes of fretfully gripped chords.

Feeling his parents' mute cheerleading
from the living room—we feigned reading—
he retreated to the basement from the den.
We eavesdropped through the cellar door.

"English speakers know that *cellar door*
is among the loveliest phrases in our tongue,
especially if detached from its sense,"
said Tolkien—not the first to say it, but

"I have a hatred of apartheid in my bones"
belongs to him alone. Ethan's milestone
was a trademark lick: *House of the Rising Sun.*
Work made play? Not quite. Songs still groped

to a halt. Dad to the marrow, I've hyped
his steps from chords to chord progressions
aspiring up the stairs. The ones he coined
he called *noodlings*—tunes stitched from bits

his hand happened on. Three years plus
our language blown to atoms: *losers, fake,
haters, failing, fire and fury*, and those two
so barefaced they spit: *excuse me; believe me . . .*

When Ethan finally added his own lyrics,
when what he wrote he sang, we listened
even closer through the cellar door—not
to a novice, but to a master, of the look.

AARON WALLACE

Battle Hymn of the Republic

God, could Kieran sing!—
when we were bunked up in a barracks
with a rotting roof and rusty pipes,
and the acoustics otherworldly.

Songs about honeysuckle and goats
made the swamp air breathable, but only
when it was Kieran singing the platoon
to sleep, only when it was our lullaby.

He told me to write. Drinking stolen Icehouse
between woolen-wrapped beds, he told me
I had no choice. So, I wrote a poem
about my ex-girlfriend's sister in a blue bikini—

he put it to an acoustic tune:
True Americana, we called it; and until August
when he drove to the woods and shot himself,
we sang it for the entire summer.

Timothy Donnelly
Julia Burgdorff

I don't know if the experience represented in "The Field" actually occurred or if it's entirely imagined. What reader can? Maybe it's a composite of real-life observations or of experience and imagination. But, what do I even mean by "experience" anyway? It's not like anything actually happens here; it's "Almost / but not quite nothing." There's pollen in the air, hummingbirds in a nonspecific bush, light, sound, wind, and then a rabbit. A scenario like this unfolds every midsummer, often without a human in it to infect it with our perspective, our need to supplement what is with our concerns. But the speaker in "The Field" doesn't interfere with the environment—she is tantamount to the rabbit, simply "watching." But watching what? The light; the vital pollen lit by it, or else "pollen" might mean yellow here, but both meanings coalesce; and of course the "jeweled disturbance" of the hummingbird—ambassadors of light, or messengers of a place made of light and luxury and air, an almost medieval brocade heaven. Think *Pearl*. But Burgdorff's instincts are to give the poem dimension by complicating it with cooler tones, notes of science and threat and strangeness like the hummingbird's "Metallic trills" that evoke (and also provoke) "nerve signals," a touch of ominousness in "The wind / is picking up," plus the surprising revelation that "The field has no entrance." These prepare for the haunting curtain at the poem's end, a simile for the trees but still a distinct presence in the poem, suggestive not simply of the theater, but of a divider between places, even dimensions. Think the Black Lodge in *Twin Peaks*. It's this sense of otherworldliness that supports the startling last couplet's most revelatory reading—the "you" is no ordinary listener (it's notably not a "who," it's a "what"), but a nonhuman spirit inherent in nature, one who might orchestrate moments like this, scenes that sensitize us to the presence of the divine, or at least to its possibility. Either way, the poet reproduces what she refers to, casting the brief spell of "The Field" onto the reader, who leaves it to rejoin the world expanded, transported, dazzled.

TIMOTHY DONNELLY

Etruscan Vase with Flowers

If ever a blue could bypass the forebrain and make its appeal
    directly to the amygdala, you are that blue. Hybrid of raincloud
and of periwinkle—not the mollusk, which is thought
    to have been brought to the Americas stuck to the rock

ballast of European trade ships, but the tint of that eponymous
    invasive ground cover whose simple blooms are known elsewhere
as the flower of death, after the ancient custom of placing
    wreaths of them on heads of dead children, or more accurately

at their feet—you leap from the ochres of everything else
    multidimensionally, like a mystic whisper in an ordinary place.
A Staples comes to mind. Strange name, seeming to mean to conjure
    essentials, yet totally overshadowed by the image of metal

fixtures forging connection via puncture and force. You understand
    how vivid specificity kills juice, obviates and thereby
sterilizes the mind's invention. You exist in opposition. You open
    with unreal flowers what the logic of prose means to close through

the hours of my existence, which diminish in number, whereas
    infinity does not. You, wordlessly, argue the feasibility
of transport, the way Redon himself told poets of his day to look
    to the sea, whose only options are unboundedness and boundlessness.

JULIA BURGDORFF

The Field

The field is full of pollen light
and the jeweled disturbance

of hummingbirds. Almost
but not quite nothing.

Metallic trills like nerve signals
in a pink-flowered bush. The wind

is picking up. It's so easy
to forget and forget.

The field has no entrance.
A rabbit on its hind legs

watching. At the edge, trees waver
like a curtain in the dark.

I don't know what I am addressing
but I've always known it's you.

Tom Sleigh

Karen Fish

The elegant, distanced, cool analytical powers of Karen Fish embody what Elizabeth Bishop meant by "the mind in motion" as opposed to the mind at rest. Her poems dramatize a process of re-evaluation and self-interrogation. The skepticism with which the speaker examines her own feelings, as well as her conflicted and conflicting versions of the past of her immediate family, widen the range of her reflections to what Czeslaw Milosz once called "the general human perspective." And what that perspective includes is the truth of family legacy; the hard give and take between (and among) men and women, married and unmarried; the way language keeps telling a different story than the one you think you're telling about family, spouse, child; and how this permeability, or porousness of language, effects our view of history, both personal and public.

Which isn't to say she's a poetic version of what might seem like quaint philosophical positions staked out thirty years ago concerning polysemy, and language as an unconscious reifier of systems of social control. Nothing she writes accepts that language is inadequate to fully capture reality. But she proceeds by making contradiction and uncertainty, embodied in her penchant for loose and periodic sentences, the main means of examining, in a wholly rigorous way, the conflicting morals, conclusions, and emotional truths that her work obsessively presents. Her syntax reminds me of a kind of fractured Henry James—instead of his fluidity, she proceeds by fits and starts: elliptical constructions, parallel series, and abruptly enjambed lines suggest how all consciousness and all choices of meaning that unfold temporally might suddenly be seen simultaneously.

Of course they can't, but cumulatively as poem after poem unfolds, there is a way in which these syntactic patterns create an artful illusion of seeing things from the eye of eternity, outside time—as in this poem I've chosen about childhood, "Kick the Can."

The poem is virtuosic in how closely her perceptions track her indecisions. And yet there's nothing indefinite or floaty about the way she formulates her doubt.

TOM SLEIGH

My Mother's Cigarettes

for my mother's 95th birthday

What was she doing? Pretending she was
smoking? Almost blind, did she know
that I was watching her empty fingers
fork into a V as she mimed lifting to her lips
with languorous movie star glamor that sexiest
of cigarettes? This woman, my mother
from a tiny Kansas Dustbowl town where she'd
heard of movies as a girl but never seen one,
flaunted that imaginary cigarette
with all the nonchalance of Bacall—one of two
I've ever seen her smoke—the first one real,
years ago, when she kissed my long dead dad
on the lips, maybe showing off in front of us,
her four-square children squeamish about what
our parents' hands and mouths were doing
as she took a long drag and blew smoke rings
orbiting one inside the other, then handed her cigarette
to my father so that he, too, took a drag
and blew smoke back—and now, this phantom drag
she takes fifty years later, her manner
fidgety, jittery, a devious little smile
on her unlipsticked lips that she used
to lipstick every day, now fiercely
other to all who knew her as deep into
her lungs she sucks ghost smoke expanding
through all her branching airways before
finally she exhales—was that the first sign
of her mind going, her memory diffusing
like those smoke rings fading lazily away?
Pupils peering right through me in her puzzled,
owlish stare, whether she's trying

to meet my eyes or gropes for my fingers
or keeps on blindly staring beyond what comes after
her and me, it's as if she has second sight
and keeps staring at a mountain, eyes boring
into its stony up-againstness. Ready
and estranged, unfazed inside her privacy,
she savors a last puff and stubs it out.

KAREN FISH

Kick the Can

A clutch of us—interchangeable.
Twelve and thirteen all too skinny, super awkward except
in silhouette and shadow sliding between the twilit hedges.
Our parents all together, being neighborly.
Their laughter a kind of distant silverware
clatter. Occasional exclamation, the laughter that comes with
drinking, talking politics and joking sex.
We couldn't have been more disinterested in them.
The hope—they would utterly forget us, forget dinner—
leaving us to run past the shadows enlarging till

the game became intrinsic to us, became us.
We ran on the promise of being swift and strategic—
loving each other in the sure-footed slip through
that liquid descent of the day. The air salmon, broad leaf
end of summer locust thrum. It was the first time
we felt part of something larger than ourselves—mirrored,
mirroring, with our shaggy hair, old sneakers, thin chests,
all arms and legs, bright eyes—
heaving and out of breath.
What we didn't quite know then
was that we might never be happier, never more
exhilarated as that big summer moon
heeled itself higher and higher ladling light.

Ye Mimi

Wu Yu Hsuan

When I asked Ye Mimi to recommend a poet, I was delighted at her suggestion of Wu Yu Hsuan, for I had been following the work of this deliciously idiosyncratic poet and essayist for some time and had in fact done a tentative translation of several of her poems, among them "A Dream of Stone." I was also delighted at the differences in their work. Whereas Mimi tends to channel her poetry and favors sound over sense, Yu Hsuan writes out of a desire to make palpable sense of some thing or idea that takes her out of herself or leaves her beside herself in wonder—or as she herself puts it: "leaves me beautifully split open." One such notion—the theme of "A Dream of Stone"—is how love, as a felt experience, seems to spread itself relentlessly, imperceptibly, over everything. I should perhaps also mention that Taiwan is extremely mountainous and volcanic. Rockfalls are quite common, and, over time, the force of gravity and wind and wave turn every stone into grains of sand.

Steve Bradburry

YE MIMI

或被

被病中或被命中或被猜中或被折衷或被熱衷或被苦衷或被
效忠或被鬧钟或被播种或被變种或被浮肿或被或被或被或
被或被或被消肿

安寧的意思就是
閒置屋內的女人用心的器皿來盛裝光潔的柳丁
不超速也不被客訴

YE MIMI translated by STEVE BRADBURY

Or Being

Being in sickness or being bullseyed or being guessed or being
compromised or being an object of obsession or one of secret
sorrow, being loyalled or alarmclocked, being sowed or subject to
variation or being bloated or being or being or being blessed by a
timely detumescence

The meaning of tranquility is
An idle woman in an idle house using the cockles of the heart to
    hold the glossy oranges
Not speeding or being sued

WU YU HSUAN

石頭夢

如果我是風
每一條岔路
我都要走看看

看看最深的山谷
留下多少迴響

名為愛的那些石頭
落下
多少還摸著日常的溪流
走成一條沒有盡頭的路
把自己變得面目全非

誰還記得入海的風
沒心沒肺
吹動一顆沙塵
遠離
山谷的迴響

WU YU HSUAN translated by STEVE BRADBURY

A Dream of Stone

were I the wind
at every turn in the road
I would want to go and see

see into the deepest valley
leave how many echoes echoing

those stones we know as love
fall
feel their way down every brook and rivulet
follow roads that know no end
altering themselves completely

who remembers the wind that went down to the sea
heartlessly
blowing a grain of sand
far
from the echoing valley

CONTRIBUTORS

Kelli Russell Agodon's news book is *Dialogues with Rising Tides* (Copper Canyon Press). She is the cofounder of Two Sylvias Press and serves on the poetry faculty at the Rainier Writing Workshop, a low-residency MFA program at Pacific Lutheran University. www.agodon.com

Nin Andrews' poems have appeared in many literary journals and anthologies including *Ploughshares*, *Agni*, *The Paris Review*, and four editions of *Best American Poetry*. The author of seven chapbooks and seven full-length poetry collections, she has won two Ohio individual artist grants, the Pearl Chapbook Contest, the Kent State University chapbook contest, the Gerald Cable Poetry Award, and the Ohioana 2016 Award for poetry. She is also the editor of a book of translations of the Belgian poet, Henri Michaux, called *Someone Wants to Steal My Name*. Her book, *The Last Orgasm*, was published by Etruscan Press in 2020.

Rae Armantrout's latest book is *Finalists* published by Wesleyan in 2022. She currently lives in the Seattle area.

Cassandra Atherton is an Australian prose poet. She co-authored *Prose Poetry: An Introduction* (Princeton UP) and her most recent book of prose poetry is *Leftovers* (Gazebo).

Tacey M. Atsitty, Diné (Navajo), is Tsénahabiłnii (Sleep Rock People) and born for Ta'neeszahnii (Tangle People). She is a PhD student in Creative Writing at Florida State University in Tallahassee, where she lives with her husband.

Emily Banks is the author of *Mother Water* (Lynx House Press, 2020) and a Visiting Assistant Professor at Emory University. Her poems have appeared in *32 Poems*, *CutBank*, *Heavy Feather Review*, *Superstition Review*, *The Cortland Review*, and other journals.

Olivia Banks is a recent graduate of Framingham State University, where she is now pursuing her Post-Baccalaureate Teacher's Licensure and Master's in Education. She enjoys writing and reading free verse poetry, and has been published in her college literary journal *The Onyx*, which she was the editor of for two years.

Madeleine Barnes is a writer, visual artist, and doctoral candidate at The Graduate Center, City University of New York. She is the author of *You Do Not Have to Be Good* (Trio House Press, 2020) and four chapbooks, and she serves as Poetry Editor at Cordella Press. madeleinebarnes.com, cordella.org

Linda Bierds' tenth book of poetry, published in 2019, is *The Hardy Tree*. She teaches at the University of Washington in Seattle.

Sophie Cabot Black has three poetry collections from Graywolf Press, *The Misunderstanding of Nature*, (Norma Farber First Book Award) and *The Descent*, (2005 Connecticut Book Award) and *The Exchange* (2013).

Deborah Bogen's books include *Landscape with Silos*, *Let Me Open You a Swan*, and most recently *In Case of Sudden Free Fall*, Jacar Press, 2017. *Speak Now This Charm* is forthcoming from Jacar Press.

Alain Borer, the author of more than thirty-five books, has received several awards, including the 70th annual Prix Apollinaire for his play *Icare & I don't* (2008), the Joseph Kessel Prize for his novel *Koba* (2003), and the 2005 Edouard Glissant Award for the entirety of his work. Long associated with the poet Arthur Rimbaud, Borer's thirty years of research have yielded ten books on his work, including *Rimbaud in Abyssinia* (Seuil, 1984), translated by Rosmarie Waldrop into English; *Arthur Rimbaud, le lieu et la formule*, Mercure de France, 1999; *Rimbaud, l'heure de la fuite*, Gallimard, 2001; along with a feature film, *le Voleur de feu* (TF1, 1978, with Leo Ferré).

Elizabeth Bradfield's most recent book is *Theorem*, a collaboration with artist Antonia Contro. Based on Cape Cod, Liz works as a naturalist, teaches at Brandeis University, and runs Broadside Press. She is co-editor with Alexandra Teague and Miller Oberman of *Broadsided Press: Fifteen Years of Poetic and Artistic Collaboration, 2005–2020*.

Steve Bradbury is a Florida-based artist, writer, and Chinese translator. His most recent collection, *Amang's Raised by Wolves: poems and conversations* (Deep Vellum, 2020), won the 2021 PEN Award for Poetry in Translation.

Julia Burgdorff lives in New York City. Her work has been published in *Recliner Magazine* and *SAND Journal*.

Elena Karina Byrne, the former Regional Director of the Poetry Society of America, works as an editor, the Programming Consultant for *The Los Angeles Times* Festival of Books, and Literary Program Director for the Ruskin Art Club. A Pushcart Prize, and Best American Poetry recipient, her books include: *If This Makes You Nervous* (Omnidawn, 2021), *No Don't* (What Books Press, 2020), *Squander* (Omnidawn, 2016), *Masque* (Tupelo Press, 2008), and *The Flammable Bird*, (Zoo Press/Tupelo Press, 2002). She's writing screenplays while completing her collection of hybrid essays entitled *Voyeur Hour*.

Nicole Callihan writes poems and stories. Her work has appeared in *Kenyon Review*, *Conduit*, *American Poetry Review*, and as a Poem-a-Day selection from the Academy of American Poets.

Rafael Campo teaches and practices internal medicine at Beth Israel Deaconess Medical Center and Harvard Medical School, where he also directs the Art and Humanities Initiative's Literature and Writing Program. He is also the Poetry Section Editor for *JAMA, the Journal of the American Medical Association*. Author of nine highly acclaimed books, his honors and awards include a Guggenheim fellowship and a Lambda Literary Award. His poetry and essays have appeared *The Nation*, *The New Republic*, *The New York Times*, *Poetry*, *Scientific American* and elsewhere. He lectures widely, with recent appearances at TEDx Cambridge, the Folger Shakespeare Library, and the Library of Congress. His new and selected volume of poems, *Comfort Measures*

Only, is now available from Duke University Press. For more information, please visit www.rafaelcampo.com.

Katerina Canyon was born and raised in Los Angeles, and she often writes of her life experiences and her childhood. She now lives in Seattle and works as a poetry workshop teacher and children's activist.

Andrei Codrescu's new book is *Miracle and Catastrophe*, a collection of Romanian interviews 1970–2021, Editura Cartier.

Cathy Colman, MFA, is a best-selling poet and journalist, winner of the Felix Pollak Prize from the University of Wisconsin. Her poetry collections include *Borrowed Dress* (University of Wisconsin), *Beauty's Tattoo* (Tebot Bach) and most recently *Time Crunch* (What Books). She has been a free-lancer for *The New York Times Book Review*.

Steven Cramer's sixth collection, *Listen*, was published by MadHat Press in 2020. His previous books include *Goodbye to the Orchard* (Sarabande, 2004) and *Clangings* (Sarabande, 2012). He founded and teaches in the Low-Residency MFA Program in Creative Writing at Lesley University.

Jim Daniels' latest book of poems is *Gun/Shy*, Wayne State University Press. Other recent books include his fiction collection, *The Perp Walk* and his anthology, *RESPECT: The Poetry of Detroit Music* (2020), co-edited with M. L. Liebler, (both from Michigan State University Press). A native of Detroit, he lives in Pittsburgh and teaches in the Alma College low-residency MFA program.

Kwame Dawes is the author of twenty-two books of poetry and numerous other books of fiction, criticism, and essays, most recently *Nebraska* and *UnHistory* (with John Kinsella). He is Director of the African Poetry Book Fund and Co-Founder of the Calabash International Literary Festival. Dawes is a Chancellor of the Academy of American Poets and a Fellow of the Royal Society of Literature. His awards include an Emmy, the Forward Poetry Prize, a Guggenheim Fellowship and the prestigious Windham Campbell Prize for Poetry.

Timothy Donnelly's fourth book of poems, *Chariot*, will be published by Wave Books in 2023. He teaches at the Columbia University School of the Arts.

Lynn Emanuel is the author of five books of poetry. Her most recent book, *The Nerve Of It: Poems New and Selected*, was awarded the Lenore Marshall Award by The Academy of American Poets. Her other awards include multiple fellowships from the National Endowment for the Arts, The National Poetry Series Award, the Eric Matthieu King Award also from The Academy of American Poets and, most recently, a fellowship from the Civitella Ranieri Foundation. She has been a judge for the National Book Awards and has taught at the Bread Loaf Writers' Conference, The Warren Wilson Program in Creative Writing, and the Bennington College Low Residency MFA program. Her poetry has been published and reviewed in *Poetry*, *The New York Times Book Review*, *The New York Times Magazine*, *The Harvard Review*, *LA Review of Books*, *BOMB Magazine*, and *Publisher's Weekly*.

Alejandro Escudé's first book of poems, *My Earthbound Eye*, was published in September 2013 upon winning the 2012 Sacramento Poetry Center Award. He received a master's degree in creative writing from UC Davis. Alejandro is a high school English teacher, having taught in a variety of school systems at the secondary level for nearly twenty years. Originally from Córdoba, Argentina, he immigrated to California many years ago at the age of six. A new collection, *The Book of the Unclaimed Dead*, published by Main Street Rag Press, is now available at mainstreetrag.com.

Karen Fish's third book, *No Chronology* was published by University of Chicago Press, Spring 2020. Her work has appeared in *The New Yorker*, *Poetry*, *The American Poetry Review*, *The New Republic* and *Slate*.

Jennifer Franklin is the author of three poetry collections including *If Some God Shakes Your House* (Four Way Books, 2023). She is the recipient of a City Artist Corps/NYFA grant in poetry, a CRCF grant in literature, and teaches poetry workshops in Manhattanville's MFA program and at the Hudson Valley Writers Center, where she is Program Director.

Daisy Fried's fourth book of poems, *The Year the City Emptied* (Flood Editions) was published in 2022. The recipient of Guggenheim, Hodder and Pew fellowships, she is a member of the faculties of the University of the Arts and the Warren Wilson MFA Program for Writers. She lives in Philadelphia.

Ramón García is the author of two books of poetry *The Chronicles* (Red Hen Press, 2015) and *Other Countries* (What Books Press, 2010), and a scholarly monograph on the artist Ricardo Valverde (University of Minnesota Press, 2013). He teaches at California State University, Northridge and lives in Los Angeles. https://ramongarciaphd.com

Ani Gjika is an Albanian-born poet, literary translator, and author of *Bread on Running Waters* (2013). She's a recipient of several awards and fellowships including the NEA, English PEN, the Robert Pinsky Global Fellowship and, most recently, Restless Books' 2021 Prize for New Immigrant Writing for her forthcoming memoir.

Beckian Fritz Goldberg is the the author of *Egypt From Space* and six previous volumes of poetry. She lives in Oxnard, California.

Adam Grabowski is the author of the chapbook *Go on Bewilderment* (Attack Bear Press, 2020) and his poems have appeared or are forthcoming in such journals as *New Ohio Review*, *Sixth Finch*, *Exit 7*, and elsewhere. He holds an MFA in Writing from the Vermont College of Fine Arts and is currently the associate managing editor for *The Maine Review*.

Yona Harvey is the author of two poetry collections, *You Don't Have to Go to Mars for Love*, winner of the Believer Book Award for Poetry and *Hemming the Water*, winner of the Kate Tufts Discovery Award. She contributed to Marvel's *World of Wakanda*, a companion series to the bestselling *Black Panther* comic, and co-wrote Marvel's *Black Panther & The Crew*. Poems previously-published—Four Way Books. Yona Harvey has just been announced as a 2022 Guggenheim Fellow.

Julie Heming is a Korean American adoptee and Academy of American Poets University & College Poetry Prize recipient. Her work has appeared in *The Oakland Review*. A graduate of Carnegie Mellon University, she currently works as a content writer outside Pittsburgh, PA.

J.J. Hernandez is a poet in Fresno, California whose work has been supported by the Community of Writers Workshop and the Fresno State Laureate Lab. He currently reads for *The Offing Magazine*, his work has been published in *Tinderbox*, *Queen Mob's Tea House*, *The Acentos Review*, *Crab Orchard Review*, *Glass: A Journal of Poetry*, *The Missouri Review*, and *The American Poetry Review*.

Juan Felipe Herrera, Poet Laureate of the United States, Emeritus. Recent book, *Everyday We Get More Illegal* (City Lights, SF). Recent Awards, Lifetime Achievement Award – UC Riverside and LA Review of Books. Lives in Fresno, CA with his partner, poet, Margarita Robles.

Bob Hicok's most recent book is *Red Rover Red Rover* (Copper Canyon Press, 2021).

Shamar Hill is Black, Cherokee, and Jewish. He is the recipient of numerous awards including fellowships from the New York Foundation for the Arts, Cave Canem, and Fine Arts Work Center. He has been published in: *American Poetry Review*, *Poetry Northwest*, *The Missouri Review*, and *Washington Square Review*, among others. He is working on a poetry collection, *Photographs of an Imagined Childhood*, and a memoir, *In Defiance of All True Things*.

Jane Hirshfield's most recent, ninth poetry collection *Ledger* (Knopf, 2020) centers on the crises of climate, biosphere, and social justice. Her work been translated into over fifteen languages. A former chancellor of the Academy of American Poets, she was elected in 2019 into the American Academy of Arts & Sciences.

Garrett Hongo is the author of *Coral Road: Poems*. Forthcoming from Pantheon Books in February is *The Perfect Sound: A Memoir in Stereo* (non-fiction). He teaches at the University of Oregon.

Mark Irwin is the author of eleven collections of poetry, including *Shimmer* (2020), *A Passion According to Green* (2017), *American Urn: Selected Poems* (1987–2014), and *Bright Hunger* (2004). Recognition for his work includes The Nation/Discovery Award, two Colorado Book Awards, four Pushcart Prizes, the James Wright Poetry Award, the Philip Levine Prize for Poetry, and fellowships from the Fulbright, Lilly, and NEA. He has also translated three volumes of poetry.

L. A. Johnson is the author of the chapbook *Little Climates* (Bull City Press, 2017) and the winner of the 2021 Rumi Prize in Poetry from *Arts & Letters*. Her poems have recently appeared or are forthcoming in *APR*, *Poetry*, *The Southern Review*, *ZYZZYVA*, and other journals.

Allen Clarence Jones lives in dark material comfort serving as associate professor of English at the University of Stavanger in southwest Norway. His novel *Her Death Was Also Water* is forthcoming from Australian publisher MidnightSun.

Carolyn Joyner's work has been featured in numerous literary journals and anthologies including *Revise the Psalm: Work Celebrating the Writing of Gwendolyn Brooks, Gathering Ground, Beyond the Frontier, Obsidian*, and *Pleiades*. She is a fellow of Cave Canem, Hurston-Wright, and the Virginia Center for the Creative Arts, and has been awarded two artist fellowship grants from the DC Commission on the Arts and Humanities. The Library of Congress featured discussion of the creation of her current manuscript collection, *Imagine His Mother Witnessing*, formerly entitled, *Bone Through Skin*, in its Poet and the Poem podcast.

Karan Kapoor is a poet based in New Delhi. When Karan was little, he wanted to be an astronaut. After a few beatings at the hands of bullies, he developed an intense fear of falling and closed spaces, so he began playing with words. A recent winner of the Red Wheelbarrow Prize (judged by Mark Doty), his poems have appeared or are forthcoming in *Rattle, Atticus Review, The Indian Quarterly, The Bombay Literary Magazine, Scroll,* and elsewhere. He is eternally oppressed by his restless leg syndrome. He loves clouds, rain, rivers, and all things water. Know him more at: https://www.karankapoor.co.in/

A native of Los Angeles, **Kai-Lilly Karpman** is currently living in New York City, pursuing an MFA at Columbia University while working for the *Columbia Journal*. She also is editor-in-chief at the literary magazine *Some Kind of Opening*.

Gerry LaFemina is the author of numerous books of poetry, fiction, and criticism, and in 2022 he will release two books—his first book of creative nonfiction, *The Pursuit: A Meditation on Happiness* and *Pop*

& Hiss: Selected Punk Poems 1990–2020. He's a professor of English at Frostburg State University, a mentor in Carlow University's MFA in creative writing, and the singer and principal song writer of The Downstrokes.

Danusha Laméris is the author of *The Moons of August* (Autumn House, 2014), and *Bonfire Opera*, (University of Pittsburgh Press, 2020), winner of the Northern California Book Award in poetry. She teaches in Pacific University's low-residency MFA program.

Ananda Lima is the author of *Mother/land* (Black Lawrence Press, 2021), winner of the Hudson Prize, and four chapbooks. Her work has appeared in *The American Poetry Review, Poets.org, Kenyon Review Online*, Gulf Coast, and elsewhere.

Sarah Luczaj is a poet, writer, translator and counsellor/therapist currently based in Glasgow. She has published a chapbook of poems, a book about Reiki, a book about an intuitive process she developed, Creative Regeneration, and numerous translations and articles.

Maurice Manning's most recent book is *Railsplitter*. He lives with his family in Kentucky.

Nathan McClain is the author of *Scale* (2017) and *Previously Owned* (2022), both from Four Way Books. He teaches at Hampshire College and serves as poetry editor for the *Massachusetts Review*.

Ata Moharreri is a first generation American, born in Rolla, MO. His mother emigrated from Minsk, Belarus and his father emigrated from Tehran, Iran. He has lived in TN, IL, MA, CA, and NY.

Carol Moldaw's most recent book is *Beauty Refracted* (Four Way Books, 2018). She lives in Santa Fe, NM and teaches privately.

Yesenia Montilla, an Afro-Latina poet & daughter of immigrants, is a CantoMundo & 2020 NYFA fellow who lives in Harlem. Her first collection *The Pink Box* was longlisted for a PEN award. Her second collection *Muse Found in a Colonized Body* is forthcoming (Four Way Books, 2022).

Miguel Murphy is the author of *Shoreditch* and two previous collections of poetry. He lives in Southern California where he teaches at Santa Monica College.

Carol Muske-Dukes' recent (ninth) book of poems, *Blue Rose* (from Penguin) was a Pulitzer Prize finalist in 2019, followed by her seventh Pushcart Prize in 2021. Her many other honors (over years) include appointment as California Poet Laureate, awards for her novels and essay collections and a prize-winning play. Guggenheim, NEA, National Book award finalist, blah blah. She retired in January after many years as USC Professor of Creative Writing/English and founder of the USC PhD Program in Creative Writing/Literature and is at work on a new essay collection entitled: *Out-Spoken.*

Stacy R. Nigliazzo is a nurse and the award-winning author of *Scissored Moon* and *Sky the Oar*. Her poems have appeared in the *Bellevue Literary Review, Beloit Poetry Journal, Ploughshares*, and *JAMA*, among other publications. She is co-poetry editor of *Pulse, Voices from the Heart of Medicine* and reviews poetry for the *American Journal of Nursing*. Her new book, *My Borrowed Face*, is due out from Press 53 later this year.

In 2021 **Dan O'Brien** published his fourth poetry collection, *Our Cancers* (Acre Books), as well as *A Story That Happens: On Playwriting, Childhood, & Other Traumas* (Dalkey Archive Press; CB Editions in the UK). He is a former Guggenheim Fellow in Drama, and twice the recipient of the PEN America Award for Drama.

Romeo Oriogun, a Nigerian poet and essayist, is the author of *Sacrament of Bodies* and three chapbooks. He won the 2017 Brunel International African Poetry Prize and was a finalist for the 2020 Lambda Prize for poetry and The Future Awards African Prize for Literature. His second collection of poetry, *Gathering of Bones*, is forthcoming in 2023.

Gregory Orr will be releasing a new collection, *Selected Books of the Beloved* with Copper Canyon Press this year. The printed poems are from another new manuscript. Orr's most recent book is *A Primer for Poets and Readers of Poetry* from W. W. Norton. His most recent poetry collection was *River Inside the River* (Norton, 2013). These poems are from a newly-completed collection.

Nathaniel Perry is the author of two books of poetry, *Long Rules* (Backwaters, 2021) and *Nine Acres* (APR/Copper Canyon, 2011).

Glorious Piner is a poet, writer, and podcaster from West Philadelphia, finishing up her senior thesis at the University of Maryland's MFA program. Her work can be read in *American Poetry Review*, *Florida Review*, *Conduit Magazine*, *Scoundrel Time*, and more!

Alycia Pirmohamed is the author of the chapbooks *Second Memory*, *Hinge*, and *Faces that Fled the Wind*, as well as the collection *Another Way to Split Water* (YesYes Books). She studied creative writing at the University of Oregon and the University of Edinburgh.

Flávia Rocha is a Brazilian writer, author of the poetry collections *Exosfera* (2021), *Um País* (2015), *Quartos Habitáveis* (2011) and *A Casa Azul ao Meio-Dia* (2005). Her poems, translations and essays appeared in a number of publications in Brazil, the U.S. and in other countries.

Martha Rhodes is the author of five poetry collections, most recently *The Thin Wall*. She is a member of the faculty of the MFA Program for Writers at Warren Wilson College and is the publisher of Four Way Books. She lives in New York City.

Clare Rossini has three books. Her poems and essays have appeared widely and are collected in numerous anthologies, including *Best American Poetry 2020*. She co-edited *The Poetry of Capital*, published by the University of Wisconsin Press in 2020. Clare is Artist-in-Residence at Trinity College in Hartford, where she teaches classes in creative writing and oversees a program that places students in Hartford public school arts classrooms.

Alan Shapiro is the author of thirteen books of poetry, two memoirs, a novel, a book of critical essays and two translations. His awards include the Kingsley Tufts Award, two NEAs, a Guggenheim and a Lila Wallace Reader's Digest Award. His newest book of poems, *Life Pig*, was published in 2016 along with a book of essays, *That Self-Forgetful Perfectly Useless Concentration*, both from University of Chicago Press.

He is the William R. Kenan, Jr. Distinguished Professor of English and Creative Writing at the University of North Carolina.

Safiya Sinclair was born and raised in Montego Bay, Jamaica. She is the author of *Cannibal*, winner of a Whiting Writers' Award, the American Academy of Arts and Letters' Metcalf Award in Literature, and the Prairie Schooner Book Prize in Poetry. She is currently an Associate Professor of Creative Writing at Arizona State University. Her memoir, *How to Say Babylon*, is forthcoming from Simon & Schuster in 2023.

Other recent poems by **Jeffrey Skinner** appear in *Ploughshares*, and the *New England, Manhattan,* and *Los Angeles Reviews*.

Tom Sleigh's many books include *The King's Touch, House of Fact, House of Ruin, Station Zed,* and *Army Cats*. His most recent book of essays, *The Land Between Two Rivers: Writing In an Age of Refugees*, recounts his time as a journalist in the Middle East and Africa. He has been a Kingsley Tufts Award winner, a Guggenheim Fellow, A Lila Wallace Award recipient, as well as having received the John Updike Award and an Individual Writer Award from the American Academy of Arts and Letters, and two NEA grants in poetry. His poems have appeared in *The New Yorker, The Atlantic, Threepenny Review, Poetry, The Southern Review, Harvard Review, Raritan, The Common* and many other magazines. He is a Distinguished Professor in the MFA Program at Hunter College.

Maggie Smith is the author of six books of poems and prose, including *Goldenrod, Good Bones,* and *Keep Moving*. Her poems and essays have appeared in *The New York Times, The New Yorker, The Southern Review, The Guardian, The Paris Review, The Washington Post,* and *The Best American Poetry*.

Brandon Som is the author of *The Tribute Horse* (Nightboat Books), winner of the Kate Tufts Discovery Award, and the chapbook *Babel's Moon* (Tupelo Press), winner of the Snowbound Prize. He currently teaches in the Literature Department at the University of California, San Diego.

Ann Townsend's collections of poetry include *Dear Delinquent* (2019), *The Coronary Garden* (2005), and *Dime Store Erotics* (1998). The recipient of a Pushcart Prize, Townsend has also been awarded an Individual Artist's Grant in Poetry from the National Endowment for the Arts.

Radu Vancu is a Romanian poet, novelist and translator. President of PEN Romania. He teaches literature at the Lucian Blaga University in Sibiu, is editor-in-chief of the *Revista Transilvania* and is the director of the Poets in Transylvania festival.

Ruy Ventura was awarded, in 1997, the National Revelation Award for Poetry from the Portuguese Writers Association. His poetry and essays have been published in Portugal, Spain, Germany, Italy, Mexico, Brazil and the United States, the last of these including his collection *How to Leave a House* translated by Brian Strang.

Rushi Vyas is the author of the forthcoming poetry collection *When I Reach for Your Pulse* (Four Way Books, 2023) and the collaborative chapbook *Between Us, Not Half a Saint* (Gasher, 2021) with Rajiv Mohabir. He currently lives in Ōtepoti Dunedin in Aotearoa New Zealand where he is a PhD candidate in literature.

Aaron Wallace is a poet who writes for the sake of others, his work an attempt at redemption for actions taken during his military service. He is also Founder and Managing Editor of Passengers Press.

Michael Waters' recent books include *Caw* (BOA Editions, 2020), *The Dean of Discipline* (University of Pittsburgh Press, 2018), and a coedited anthology, *Border Lines: Poems of Migration* (Knopf, 2020). Recipient of fellowships from the Guggenheim Foundation, National Endowment for the Arts, and Fulbright Foundation, he lives in Ocean, NJ.

Zoë Ryder White's poems have appeared in *Tupelo Quarterly*, *Salamander*, *Thrush*, *Plume*, *Sixth Finch*, and *Threepenny Review*, among others. Her most recent chapbook, *Hyperspace*, is now available from Factory Hollow Press.

Michelle Whittaker, a West Indian-American poet, pianist, and university instructor, has published work in *The New York Times Magazine, The New Yorker, upstreet, Southampton Review, Narrative, Vinyl Poetry*, and other journals. Her debut book, *Surge*, is available from great weather for MEDIA.

David Wojahn's latest collection of poetry, *For the Scribe*, was issued this year from the University of Pittsburgh Press. His previous collection, *World Tree*, was published by Pitt in 2011, and was the winner of the Academy of American Poets' Lenore Marshall Prize, as well as the Poets' Prize.

Grażyna Wojcieszko is a Polish poet who has published numerous collections of poems and, in 2020, released an album, *Don't Talk About Love*. A former project manager at the European Commission, her recent work lies at the intersections of poetry, music and film.

Cecilia Woloch is an American poet, an NEA fellowship recipient and the author of six collections of poems and a novel. She is currently teaching as a Fulbright fellow at the University of Rzeszów in southeastern Poland.

Wu Yu Hsuan is a Taiwanese poet, dancer, and educator who has chosen to live among the Ami or Pangcah, one of Taiwan's indigenous matrilineal tribes as a way of getting closer to nature and becoming more "human," which is meaning of the word Pangcah. Although still very young, she has published many volumes of poetry and photo essays.

Ye Mimi is a Taiwanese poet, filmmaker, and "Poetry Tarot" spiritual counselor. A graduate of the Chicago Art Institute's MFA Program in Film, Video and New Media, she has garnered numerous awards for her poetry films and poetry collections, the most recent of which is titled *With/out a Hitch* which includes her marvelous chapbook, *The Ringing of the Rain Has a Forgiving Grace*.

plume poetry 10